Mary Jo Clouse is not ashamed of the gospel. In fact, wherever you encounter her, her love for Jesus Christ just spills out. She is passionate about freedom and hope, and she rejoices when God's truth rules in the lives of His people.

However, she is troubled whenever she witnesses a child of God settling for less than total liberation from the power of the enemy in every area of life. On occasions such as this, you'll see a very different kind of passion because she is persuaded that having the Spirit of God inside us means that we don't live wasteful lives—enslaved to sin, regret, pain and unforgiveness.

Often I've seen her seek out the one individual who appears to be struggling, in order to pray powerfully for his or her deliverance. I admire Mary Jo very much. I see in her a woman who is fully persuaded that there is no situation God's truth can't transform and no life His love can't redeem.

There is wisdom here—practical and profound. Mary Jo's message is worthy of your attention. If you approach this book prayerfully and with an open heart, you can expect to be changed.

—BRENDA J. DAVIS
EDITOR, *SpiritLed Woman*

Mary Jo Clouse is a powerful minister in deliverance with the love of Christ. In Finland, we have seen many people suffering from sickness, demon possession and generational curses healed and set free through her ministry. I warmly recommend Mary Jo and her message in this book to be received to minister to the body of Christ all over the world.

—REV. GLORY BACKMAN
FOUNDER AND PRESIDENT, GLOBAL POWER EVANGELISM

Getting
Free

....

Getting
Free

MARY JO CLOUSE

CREATION
HOUSE
PRESS

GETTING FREE by Mary Jo Clouse
Published by Creation House Press
A part of Strang Communications Company
600 Rinehart Road
Lake Mary, Florida 32746
www.creationhouse.com

Unless otherwise noted, all Scripture quotations are from the New King James Version of the Bible. Copyright © 1979, 1980, 1982 by Thomas Nelson, Inc., publishers. Used by permission.

Scripture quotations marked KJV are from the King James Version of the Bible.

Scripture quotations marked NIV are from the Holy Bible, New International Version. Copyright © 1973, 1978, 1984, International Bible Society. Used by permission.

Scripture quotations marked AMP are from the Amplified Bible, Old Testament copyright © 1965, 1987 by the Zondervan Corporation. The Amplified New Testament copyright © 1954, 1958, 1987 by the Lockman Foundation. Used by permission.

Copyright © 2001 by Mary Jo Clouse
All rights reserved
Library of Congress Catalog Card Number: 00-108603
International Standard Book Number: 0-88419-775-1 (paperback)

1 2 3 4 5 6 7 BP 8 7 6 5 4 3 2 1
Printed in the United States of America

Acknowledgments

This book came about due to the encouragement of Joy Strang, financial director of Strang Communications, as well as the urging of my many friends and co-workers at *Charisma* and *SpiritLed Woman* magazines. They have been a real blessing in my life, and I am eternally grateful for each and every one of them.

I would also like to acknowledge my four beautiful grandchildren, Kaycee, Trent, Evan, and Ian Pope. I had them in mind as I followed God's instructions to break generational curses off me and my descendants, so they would not have to deal with generational issues. May the blessings of God almighty rest upon them, as well as future generations.

I would also like to thank and acknowledge a church in Van Buren, Arkansas, 43 Assembly of God, pastored by Randy Craig. The pastor as well as the entire congregation have been most encouraging to me during the process of getting this book published. May God's favor shine on that part of the body of Christ and His blessing continue to pour out on them.

Contents

Foreword

by Stephen Strang

The Bible says we wrestle not against flesh and blood, but against principalities and powers. Yet most Christians are oblivious about those principalities and powers or what to do about them.

That's why a book like this is important. Mary Jo Clouse is someone who has studied the Word of God to learn the principles about deliverance and has ministered successfully in this area for many years.

I have personally known Mary Jo and her husband, George, since 1973. Each of them has had a great impact on me and on my family. For a number of years, my wife, Joy, and I were in their home fellowship group, and we have remained good friends ever since.

Since 1991, Mary Jo has served as a part of our staff at Strang Communications. When we hold conferences each year, she is also an important part of our ministry team, primarily in the area of prayer and deliverance. Over the years she has become a popular workshop speaker at the annual *Charisma* Women's Conference.

So when I endorse Mary Jo's ministry, I do so with the confidence that she is a woman of God who understands this important issue and whose ministry has stood the test of time.

The area of deliverance is so important, but not readily understood. Start a conversation about confronting demons and some people will roll their eyes, saying you have gone too far out on a limb. Some will accuse you of looking for a demon under every rock. Others will tell you how they were scarred by a horrible experience when, desperate for answers, they submitted to deliverance ministry, only to have people encourage them to "vomit up" demons and do all sorts of strange things during a grueling "deliverance" session.

Others will say they are experts in the deliverance field. Some Christians believe that raising the decibel level of their prayers will chase away more demons. They have a great desire to yell at the enemy, but they lack understanding of spiritual authority. They might scream at demons all day long with no results.

I have seen and heard much in the area of deliverance. While I know deliverance is sometimes handled poorly or even arrogantly, I do believe there is an aspect of spiritual warfare to many human problems. Paul clearly states this:

> "We use God's mighty weapons, not mere worldly weapons, to knock down the Devil's strongholds. With these weapons we break down every proud argument that keeps people from knowing God. With these weapons we conquer their rebellious ideas, and we teach them to obey Christ."
> —2 CORINTHIANS 10:4–5, HOLY SPIRIT ENCOUNTER BIBLE

There are Christians who do not want to believe they can have demonic problems. I personally believe that a problem that will not go away after prayer, positive confession, fasting, strong-willed determination or medical treatment must have a demonic basis that needs to be dealt with spiritually. Problems that are hard to deal with, such as rage, drug addiction and even sexual addictions or alcoholism, have, I believe, other problems at their root. There may be strongholds in the mind and soul that must be dealt with, as well as the sinful habit or behavior that is being acted out. Let me give an important disclaimer. Some very odd behaviors are caused by medical conditions that can be treated with medicine, and I believe a doctor should be consulted to rule this out as a possible cure. If the problem continues, then it may be spiritual in nature, and deliverance may help.

Some people disagree on this issue. They feel that deliverance is not central to the gospel or is a ministry that ended in Bible times. But if you look at the ministry of Jesus, the subject of deliverance is unavoidable; you bump into it on nearly every page of the Gospels. Time and time again, Jesus confronted demons and set people free, and He also instructed His disciples to do the same.

I firmly believe that His ministry is the same today as it was then—to save, heal, deliver and preach the gospel of the kingdom. And Jesus said that casting out demons in His name would be one of the signs accompanying those of us who believe. (See Mark 16:17.)

Do you want to get free from that thing that keeps you from being the person you know God wants you to be? Are you hungry—starving for more of God? Then allow His work of deliverance to take place in your life. God really does want to meet you face to face in a glorious encounter of power. He will quench your inner thirst and remove any barriers to an intimate relationship with Him. His power will break off any bondages or hindrances keeping you from reaching your destiny in Christ.

—STEPHEN STRANG, PUBLISHER
Charisma MAGAZINE

Preface

A Medical Doctor Reports
by Margaret Chang, M.D.

In 1998, I attended the *Charisma* Women's Conference for the first time. I had recently rededicated my life to the Lord and was hungry to hear more about God, so I attended this conference. I chose a workshop called "Getting Free From Generational Curses" by Mary Jo Clouse. What a surprise that was. I had been raised in a denominational church and saved over twenty years, but I had never seen a real-live miracle.

When I entered this workshop I sensed something different. Near the end of the teaching, which in itself was different from any I had ever heard, things began to happen that I had never seen before. Ladies all around were getting healed of back problems, many of them even before they were prayed for or anyone laid hands on them. I listened with astonishment as bones in the vertebral column popped back into alignment. Ladies who had been crippled and in pain for years by disease and because of surgery began to first stand erect and then bend and touch their toes (an impossible feat just thirty minutes earlier). What an exciting time!

My first thought was, *If this could only happen for my patients.* You see, as a medical doctor of family practice, I see countless patients with back problems each day. Even after strong medication, physical therapy, steroid injections, or even major surgery, the problem remains. Seldom had I seen a complete healing, yet this was happening here. What a miracle!

I was immediately reminded of the scripture in Jeremiah 8:11: "For they have healed the hurt of the daughter of My people slightly." In the margin of my Bible the word *slightly* is also translated *superficially.* So many times I have slight recoveries in my hurting patients, and I deeply yearned to see them totally healed.

I crowded closer as Mary Jo started laying hands on ladies and commanding them to be healed in the name of Jesus. To appease my intellectual mind, I was almost crowding other people out, because I wanted to see everything up close and with my own eyes. I even got her to pray for me, and then I fell and rested in the Spirit for a real refreshing from the Lord. Since that day the two of us have become close friends, and she has prophesied over me many times. She is believing with me for a powerful ministry of both the medical and the spiritual components, completely united, to bring God's total healing for each patient. Praise God!

Part 1

....

Revelation
of
Curses

CHAPTER 1

Revelation of Generational Curses

Three of my siblings died premature deaths. But I didn't expect to have any of their health problems. After all, my husband and I were saved and on our way to heaven. Wasn't that all that was required to live a healthy life?

Yet, after my first two siblings went to be with the Lord, I developed blood sugar imbalances and heart irregularities. These problems were all-too-familiar, for my sister, Evelyn, died of complications from sugar diabetes at age forty-eight, and my brother John David, died of a heart attack at forty-four. (Later, my brother Carl passed away at fifty-eight, also from a heart attack.)

I began to wonder what was going on. I read through the Bible every year, taught Sunday school at my church, and shared my faith at every opportunity. I spent a lot of time in prayer, read books about forgiveness and, in general, was trying to live a holy life. I really felt like I was following God's instructions for a healthy life.

Immediately I went to the Lord for healing, and He delivered me from these attacks of the enemy, but I couldn't understand why I had been subject to them in the first place.

God led me to read Deuteronomy 28 and there I found my answer— I was under a curse. This was the first time I understood the existence of generational curses, and this revelation opened the door to the truths you will read on these pages.

Because of this curse, I was being attacked by a familiar spirit of infirmity. But I needed to learn how the enemy got an open door to operate in my life and my body, for it says in Proverbs 26:2, "Like a flitting sparrow, like a flying swallow, so a curse without cause shall not alight." A curse doesn't just happen: it must have a cause. What was the cause? Deuteronomy 28 again held the answer:

> But it shall come to pass, if you do not obey the voice of the Lord your God, to observe carefully all His commandments and His statutes which I command you today, that all these curses will come upon you and overtake you."
>
> —v. 15

Whenever a curse is operating in a person's life, there is a root of sin. My next thought was to find the sin in my life, though I felt that I was personally walking in obedience. Still, Proverbs 26:2 told me that "a curse without cause shall not alight."

Through study of the Word, I learned that the consequences of the sins of the fathers are visited upon the children "to the third and fourth generations" (Exod. 20:5). Just as you can have a family history of physical ailments such as heart disease, high blood pressure, diabetes and so on, you can have a family history of spiritual attacks that are the result of the sins of your ancestors.

Premature death is one outgrowth of a curse. I believe that my two brothers and my sister all succumbed early because of my grandparents' involvement in Freemasonry, a secret society that encourages practices contrary to the Word of God. After my first two siblings died, I too faced premature death. I even experienced a heart attack—the result of a generational curse still in operation. As I searched the Word of God, I learned that I had to take action to break this generational curse.

Shortly after Carl, my last remaining brother, died (ten years after John David passed away), I had my annual physical. To the doctor's surprise, my EKG was normal. Previous tests had indicated the presence of scar tissue from the heart attack.

Once I had recognized the cause of the curse, I was able to be set free of its effects. The devil could no longer pass down illness via my bloodline! Now I walk in the blessing of divine health.

As God showed me my problem and as I continued to study His Word, I learned a multitude of facts about generational curses and demons that are associated with them. I learned:

- the sources of generational curses
- types of familiar spirits
- how to identify a generational curse in your life
- how to stop a curse against you and your descendants
- how to start a blessing for you and your descendants
- how to know when forgiveness is the key to prosperity and healing
- how to use the name of Jesus
- the baptism of fire

In the past, many of us thought that when we got saved all our problems would be over. Far from it. This only gives us the beginning. Salvation gives us the revelation of how to continue getting free. You will notice this book is titled *Getting Free,* not *Get Free.* I have used this tense of get on purpose, for I feel we continually move toward the total freedom God wants for us. (journey) —

Now let us look at what allows a curse to operate, or have an effect, in our lives.

OPENING THE DOOR TO A CURSE

It is important to understand that demons cannot enter at will; they must have a legal right or gateway of opportunity. Therefore, no one can put a curse on you unless there is an opening in your life. When God's conditions have been met, a demon has no right to stay. But let's get down to some basics that God has revealed through His Word.

There are three words that people use interchangably, but each one means an entirely specific thing. First, there is *sin,* which means "to miss the mark or fall below the mark to which God has called you as an individual." Second, there is *transgression,* which means "to trespass or overstep pre-established boundaries." An example is to violate a "No Trespassing" sign by entering onto property without permission.

The third word is *iniquity,* which means "to bend or to distort the heart, a certain weakness or predisposition toward a certain sin." If a sin is repeatedly committed, it becomes an iniquity that can be passed down through the bloodline. When a person continually transgresses the law, iniquity is created in him, and that iniquity is passed to the children. Iniquity can be defined as "faulty, perverse, unjust, unrighteous, morally wrong, bowed down,

5

[handwritten: repeating the same sin over + over]

crooked, bent, etc." Iniquity is an inborn leaning or urging or bent to go a certain direction or trod a particular path. An iniquity can be considered a generational curse.

THE NATURE OF INIQUITIES

Proverbs 26:2 says, "A curse without cause shall not alight . . ."

There are certain birds that nest in Alaska and winter in Central America. They have no map but return each year to their nesting grounds in Alaska, brought back by an inborn guidance system, just as an inborn iniquity in us guides us to do certain things that we do not intentionally pursue.

There is another bird that builds a hanging nest in one of the far eastern islands. Scientists have taken eggs and brought them to America and hatched them in incubators. Even so, as the birds grow up they will build nests identical to the hanging nests of their parents, even though they have never seen them. Why? They have an inborn urging.

Iniquity is a generational curse because it predisposes us to sin and therefore gives Satan the ability to harass us. An inborn iniquity often remains hidden until it is brought forth by circumstances of life. It's like a fault in the crust of the earth. A fault is a hidden crack or imperfection that at times of stress cause major difficulties. When an earthquake comes, the location of the fault becomes visible to all. David wrote, "Cleanse thou me from secret faults . . ." (Ps. 19:12–14, KJV).

[handwritten: Sick as our Secrets]

THE CURE FOR INIQUITY

The Old Testament gives us a pattern for stopping

iniquity through God's instructions for atonement.

On the Day of Atonement, Aaron was to sacrifice one bull and two goats. The bull was a sin offering for himself and for his house.

One of the goats was sacrificed as a sin offering for the people. The second goat, however, was not killed. Instead, Aaron was instructed to "lay both his hands on the head of the live goat, *confess over it all the iniquities* of the children of Israel, and all their transgressions, concerning all their sins, putting them on the head of the goat, and shall send it away in the wilderness" (italics added). This was the scapegoat. This is where the word *scapegoat* came from: the one who takes the blame.

Surely he has borne our griefs and carried our sorrow; Yet we esteemed Him stricken, Smitten by God, and afflicted. But He was wounded for our transgressions. He was bruised for our iniquities; The chastisement for our peace was upon Him, And by his stripes we are healed. All we like sheep have gone astray; We have turned, every one, to his own way; And the Lord has laid on Him the iniquity of us all. he was oppressed and He was afflicted, yet He opened not His mouth; He was led as a lamb to the slaughter, And as a sheep before its shearers is silent. So he opened not His mouth. He was taken from prison and from judgment, And who will declare His generation? For He was cut off from the land of the living; For the transgressions of My people He was stricken. And they made His grave with the wicked—But with the rich at His death, Because He had done no violence. Nor was any deceit in His mouth. Yet it pleased the Lord to bruise Him; . . . He shall prolong His days. And the pleasure of the Lord shall prosper in His hand. He

shall see the labor of His soul, and be satisfied. By
His knowledge My righteous Servant shall justify
many, For He shall bear their iniquities.

—ISAIAH 53:4–11

Jesus fulfilled all the patterns used on the Day of
Atonement, according to Isaiah 53. First, His blood was
shed for and cleansed priests and their families.
Christians today are like the priests of the Old Testament.
Although they need atonement for sin, they are not will-
fully practicing sin. Second, His blood was shed for the
common people so sinners might be saved as well, for it
cleansed their transgressions and sins. Third, He was the
scapegoat for He carried all iniquities, transgressions,
and sins, far away, into the sea of forgetfulness.

Now, since we have established the pattern that God
sets forth in the Old Testament, let's bring it down to the
present and see what we are to do. Aaron was told to confess the iniquities on the head of the live goat (who was
the scapegoat) and to send the goat and the iniquities
away. Jesus died on the cross for each of us, so therefore
He is the Scapegoat. How do we put our iniquities on the
Scapegoat? We confess them, and Jesus carries them
away. (See Leviticus 16:22; Isaiah 53:66.)

For starters, what did we do to get saved? We recognized our need for a Savior, confessed Jesus as Lord,
believed in our heart that He was raised from the dead,
and then we were saved (Rom. 10:8–9). How do we get
free from our iniquities? Very much the same way. The
first necessary step is to recognize the fact that we have
iniquities in our lives through confession. Next, we must
take away the cause (so they will not return when we
have gotten rid of them). This is followed by praying a
prayer of release so Jesus can take them away and bury
them in the sea of forgetfulness.

8

After I learned the nature of iniquity, I could see that it was the source of my problems. As soon as I realized this, I started the search to see where iniquity entered my life. As I discovered sins in my ancestors' lives, I confessed them, asking God to forgive and forget. I starting breaking those cycles that had been coming in, generation by generation, and renouncing any involvement that any of my ancestors might have had, as well as any I might have been caught up in. Leviticus 16:21 said "concerning all their sins," and I certainly didn't want to leave any of them out. After I confessed and renounced them, I prayed that God would release me.

SPIRITUAL BLOODLINES

I understood where my heart and blood sugar problems originated. But it took several years before we recognized the origin of a problem that occurred shortly after we were married. About two years after we were married, I had a hysterectomy. The doctor forewarned me that I could have cancer, and though we had prepared for the worst, still we prayed for the best for we were brand-new Christians at that time. The surgery was successful, and tests that were run afterward said there were no cancerous cells in my body.

One thing that we thought about later was, why were there signs of cancer? There had been no cancer in my bloodline. Then suddenly the awful truth dawned on us. My husband's mother had died of cancer when he was only eight years old. Iniquities from her generation were following the bloodline. How can that be? First, let me answer by telling you a little about the marriage covenant.

When a man and woman come together, it is a covenant. Father God planned it that way and told us in Genesis that it would be so. One man and one woman make one, according to God. You would think that one half and one half make a whole, according to what we have been taught in math. That is not true when it comes to marriage. One half of a man and one half of a woman do not make a whole. They make one half, with many problems.

When my husband and I got married, we were not saved. Therefore, we were joined in body and soul, but not in spirit (for our spirits were *not* born again). Because of that, when we consummated our marriage, our generational curses flowed from him to me and from me to him.

Since we did not know at that time anything about generational curses, the demonic forces had an inroad into both of our lives. He passed his generational curse of cancer to me, and I passed my generational curse of heart problems to him. (He later had a heart problem and we rebuked the devil and got rid of that curse).

As we matured as Christians and got a revelation of generational curses, we each repented of passing things to each other. We rededicated ourselves to each other, this time in *spirit, soul* and *body.* Even though we loved each other dearly and had a great marriage for the first two years, we were only two-thirds married. Now we are completely complete in all things. Praise God!

We have been married now for over thirty years and are still discovering facets of marriage that we did not know about. One of our issues dealt with submission. For many years we tried to fit in a mold like other people said, and still we just could not seem to justify each situation. Then one day God revealed to us that submission really means "to come under the protection of"! I have no problem with that definition. I think God made the man to be the protector and woman to enjoy that protection. Today in America we have gotten so strong on the equal rights of women that a woman can hardly submit to the protection of a man.

I pray that you, too, have received the revelation of generational curses. It is extremely difficult to get rid of anything you do not have a revelation of. I always say that "you can have anything that you believe it is God's will for you to have, or you can get rid of anything you believe it is God's will for you to be set free of!" So get your revelation going and operate in faith to set your believer in motion as well.

Now that you are aware of generational curses, let's look at how you can tell whether a generational curse is operating in your life.

CHAPTER 2

Signs of a Generational Curse

A wide variety of conditions can indicate that a curse could be working in your life. I am going to list seven of the most common conditions as well as the words that people say in those circumstances. As you read these descriptions, check your life and see if the pattern fits.

1. Mental or emotional breakdown.
"It's driving me crazy!"
"I just can't take anymore."
"It makes me mad to think . . ."

2. Repeated or chronic sicknesses, especially if the illnesses are hereditary or without clear medical diagnosis.
"Whenever there's a bug, I catch it."
"I'm sick and tired . . ."
"It runs in the family, so I guess I'm the next one on the list."

There are certainly familiar spirits of infirmity that follow from generation to generation and cause many problems. One example of a spirit of infirmity is described in Luke 13:11–13: "And behold, there was a woman who had a spirit of infirmity eighteen years, and was bent over and could in no way raise herself up."

3. Repeated miscarriages or related female problems or barrenness.

"I don't think I'll ever get pregnant!"

"I've got the 'curse' again."

"I just know I'm going to lose this one — I always do!"

4. Continuing financial insufficiency, especially where the income appears sufficient.

"I never can make ends meet — my father was the same way."

"I can't afford to tithe."

"I hate those 'fat cats' who get all they ever want — it never happens to me."

5. Breakdown of marriage and family alienation.

"The palm reader said my husband would leave me."

"Somehow, I always knew my husband would find another woman."

"In our family we have always fought like cats and dogs."

6. Being accident prone.

"It always happens to me!"

"I knew there was trouble ahead . . ."

"I'm just a clumsy kind of person."

7. A history of suicides or unnatural deaths in the family.

"What's the use of living?"

"Over my dead body."

"I'd rather die than go on the way I am."

Here are some secondary indications of a curse.

1. Disturbed sleep
2. Nightmares
3. Headaches
4. Generational alcoholism
5. Depression / Daddy
6. A rash of accidents
7. Unexplainable fatigue
8. Suicidal thoughts
9. Memory lapses / anger
10. Hampered breathing
11. Outbursts of anger
12. Heart palpitations
13. Premature death (especially running in one gender of the family)

Many times when a generational curse is in operation, you reach a certain pinnacle of success in your life and then you seem to slip back. You pick yourself up and start over, but again and again things go wrong. You often have a sense of being frustrated and never quite succeeding at whatever you try to do.

Do you see where some curses might be working in your life? The first step to bring about change is to recognize that something in your life is wrong. You will never get free unless you recognize the need to get free. The next step is to make the decision to make the needed change. God is so good that He gives us the power to make the change, but He requires us to make the decision.

CONDITIONS FOR BLESSINGS

There are three ways that a spirit or curse can attach itself to you. First, there is a word curse. A word curse comes into our lives through words spoken, either by ourselves or someone else. The second way a curse can come upon us is through a "soulish curse," and the third way is through an iniquity. I want to deal with iniquity now. To do this, we will have to go back to Deuteronomy 28 and read the instructions that God gave His people through Moses as they prepared to inhabit the Promised Land.

First, God described the blessings that He had in store for His people (verses 1–14).

> Now it shall come to pass, if you diligently obey the voice of the LORD your God, to observe carefully all His commandments which I command you today, that the LORD your God will set you high above all nations of the earth. [Notice that God wants obedience from His people.]
> And all these blessings shall come upon you and overtake you, because you obey the voice of the LORD your God: [Notice again that God insists on obedience.] "Blessed shall you be in the city, and blessed shall you be in the country. Blessed shall be the fruit of your body, [your offspring] the produce of your ground [your work] and the increase of your herds, the increase of your cattle and the off-spring of your flocks. [This means your net worth will increase and you will prosper.].
> "Blessed shall be your basket and your kneading bowl. Blessed shall you be when you come in, and blessed shall you be when you go out. The LORD will cause your enemies who rise against you to be

15

defeated before your face; they shall come out against you one way and flee before you seven ways." [When God says "blessed," He actually means multiplication. He is not a God who adds to; He is a God who multiplies. When we are blessed we receive bountifully many times more than what we have given out. What a concept!]

"The LORD will command the blessing on you in your storehouses and in all to which you set your hand, and He will bless you in the land which the LORD your God has given you. The LORD will establish you as a holy people to Himself, just as He has sworn to you, if you keep the commandments of the LORD your God and walk in His ways." [Again, notice that He promises the blessings if we stay in obedience. This means us today, just as surely as it meant the children of Israel then!]

"Then all peoples of the earth shall see that you are called by the name of the LORD, and they shall be afraid of you. And the LORD will grant you plenty of goods, in the fruit of your body, in the increase of your livestock, in the produce of your ground, in the land of which the LORD swore to your fathers to give you. The LORD will open to you His good treasure, the heavens, to give the rain to your land in its season, and to bless all the work of your hand. You shall lend to many nations, but you shall not borrow. [Notice that He says he will *bless all the work of your hand.* That one blessing will change your life if you can latch on to it and stay in obedience to Him!]

"And the LORD will make you the head and not the tail; you shall be above only, and not be beneath, if you heed the commandments of the

LORD your God, which I command you today, and are careful to observe them. So you shall not turn aside from any of the words which I command you this day, to the right or the left, to go after other gods to serve them."

CONDITIONS FOR CURSES

Now, as we read the rest of Deuteronomy 28, starting with verse 15, we find out what curses come on when we do not obey the voice of the Lord. Let's read a few verses and see just what He means:

"But it shall come to pass, if you do not obey the voice of the LORD your God, to observe carefully all His commandments and His statutes which I command you today, that all these curses will come upon you and overtake you:

"Cursed shall you be in the city, and cursed shall you be in the country. Cursed shall be your basket and your kneading bowl. Cursed shall be the fruit of your body and the produce of your land, the increase of your cattle and the offspring of your flocks.

"Cursed shall you be when you come in, and cursed shall you be when you go out. The LORD will send on you cursing, confusion, and rebuke in all that you set your hand to do, until you are destroyed and until you perish quickly, because of the wickedness of your doings in which you have forsaken Me.

"The LORD will make the plague cling to you until He has consumed you from the land which you are going to possess. The LORD will strike you with consumption, with fever, with inflammation,

with severe burning fever, with the sword, with
scorching, and with mildew; they shall pursue you
until you perish."

—vv. 15–22

FOR GENERATIONS

God's punishment for disobedience is firm. Yet there
are times, as in my life, when we walk in obedience, yet
we still experience the curse. I had a hard time understanding this until I read Numbers 14:18: "The Lord is
longsuffering and abundant in mercy, forgiving iniquity
and transgression; but He by no means clears the guilty,
visiting the iniquity of the fathers on the children to the
third and fourth generation." As you can see, a curse can
come from the disobedience of your ancestors.

Some people have asked me, "Now, wait just a minute.
Does that mean I have to suffer for what was done four
generations back?" What that verse means is that the
iniquity goes down to the third and fourth generation,
with the curse of the iniquity on the ones in disobedience.
Then, if they do not repent, since the iniquity is on them,
it goes down to the fourth generation, and so on for
many, many years.

Many people have said to me, "That's not fair! Curses
and iniquity came on me for what someone else did. I do
enough bad on my own without suffering for what my
ancestors did, too." That is true, but you need to look at
the positive side of it. All you have to do is repent of the
sins of your ancestors and God said in Numbers 14:18
that He would forgive iniquity and transgression. But we
must repent to get forgiveness. We are told in 1 John 1:9,
"If we confess our sins, He is faithful and just to forgive
us our sins and to cleanse us from all unrighteousness."
He will always forgive our own sins when we confess.

Likewise, He will forgive the sins of our ancestors and cancel the effects they have on us when we confess their sins and ask forgiveness.

There are other positive aspects to the principle of generations. For example, 1 Chronicles 16:14–16 says, "He is the LORD our God; His judgments are in all the earth. Remember His covenant forever, the word which He commanded, for a thousand generations, the covenant which He made with Abraham." Wow! What a promise that is. The Word says that the curses go down to the fourth generation but the blessings go down to the thousandth generation. I like that kind of promise. We find further encouragement in the New Testament: "That the blessing of Abraham might come upon the Gentiles in Christ Jesus, that we might receive the promise of the Spirit through faith . . . And if you are Christ's, then you are Abraham's seed, and heirs according to the promise" (Gal. 3:14, 29). This tells us that the covenant He made with Abraham is in reality in effect today with each of us, affirming that we really are included in the promise of blessing.

SPECIFIC CURSES

Because God's covenants with Abraham now apply to us, we must learn more about the truths of Deuteronomy 28. In verses 21 and 22 we are told that disobedience brings a spirit of infirmity from all kinds of sicknesses. As long as we are bound by this curse that could be handed down by our ancestors, then that familiar spirit will hang on to us.

Let's read a little further in verse 23: "And your heavens which are over your head shall be bronze, and the earth which is under you shall be iron." This describes the prayer life of a great part of America today.

Getting Free

I have heard people say, "When I pray, it just seems like the heavens are brass, and it all bounces back like 'sounding brass and clanging cymbals.'" Why are our prayers not answered more readily in the church? I think it is because we have not heeded the warning of this verse. Many of our churches are operating in carnal leadership instead of the true anointing of God. The touch of God must be on what is transpiring in the church to bring about a lasting change. When the breakthrough comes, then revival comes, and God's blessings pour out in a marvelous way.

Continuing in verses 24–30 the list of curses goes on:

> "The LORD will change the rain of your land to powder and dust; from the heaven it shall come down on you until you are destroyed. The LORD will cause you to be defeated before your enemies; you shall go out one way against them and flee seven ways before them; and you shall become troublesome to all the kingdoms of the earth. Your carcasses shall be food for all the birds of the air and the beasts of the earth, and no one shall frighten them away.
>
> "The LORD will strike you with the boils of Egypt, with tumors, with the scab, and with the itch, from which you cannot be healed. The LORD will strike you with madness and blindness and confusion of heart. And you shall grope at noonday, as a blind man gropes in darkness; you shall not prosper in your ways; you shall be only oppressed and plundered continually, and no one shall save you. You shall betroth a wife, but another man shall lie with her; you shall build a house, but you shall not dwell in it; you shall plant a vineyard, but shall not gather its grapes."

Confusion

One of the curses listed in verse 20, as well as 28, is confusion. I find as I talk with many Christians each year there is confusion in their lives. Confusion does not come from God. If you constantly change your mind about what you are to do or where you are to go, this could be a sign that a curse is operating in your life.

As I was reading James recently the Lord pointed out to me these verses: "If any of you lacks wisdom, let him ask of God, who gives to all liberally and without reproach, and it will be given to him. But let him ask in faith, with no doubting, for he who doubts is like a wave of the sea driven and tossed by the wind. For let not that man suppose that he will receive anything from the Lord; he is a double-minded man, unstable in all his ways" (James 1:5–8).

As is my practice, when God shows me something, I contemplate it. The Word says that if we doubt then we become double-minded. Being double-minded affects our souls, since the mind is a part of the soul, along with our will and emotions. So being double-minded could make someone a double-souled person. Believe me, that would bring on confusion. One part of the soul would be listening for God to speak (and then the other part of the soul would speak and we would be convinced that it was God). This would bring on major deception and confusion.

The Unrighteous Prosper

Have you ever complained about how sinners in the world seem to prosper more than us Christians? Deuteronomy 28:43 lists this as one of the curses:

> "The alien who is among you shall rise higher
> and higher above you, and you shall come down

21

> lower and lower. He shall lend to you, but you shall
> not lend to him, he shall be the head, and you shall
> be the tail."

Immediately afterward, God reiterates the cause in verse 45:

> "Moreover all these curses shall come upon you
> and pursue and overtake you, until you are
> destroyed, because you did not obey the voice of
> the LORD your God, to keep His commandments
> and His statutes which He commanded you."

God will not be mocked, and He has given us the solution to all our problems in His Word. The problem lies with us. We just have not taken the time to search His Word diligently and find out exactly why some of these things are coming on us.

INIQUITIES IN MY FAMILY

In obedience to the Word of God, my husband and I searched in our lives for answers for our own problems, including a major problem in financial areas. My husband grew up in poverty during the Great Depression of the 1920s and 1930s. As an adult, he always worked hard, but he never seemed to get much beyond a bare living. A saying among his family had always been, "We don't have any money, but we still have our pride and don't take charity." If you ask any of them how they are, they say "OK, just barely got enough to eat."

As we studied about iniquities we realized that his financial problems came from word curses. Words are like containers, and they come up out of your belly, "Out of the innermost part of the belly [our heart] the mouth speaks"

(Luke 6:45). By the time the words of your heart come forth out of your mouth they are spirits. In effect, these spirits are encapsulated in little packages, whether they be good or evil. These packages go out into your home, and as the burst, they either release blessings or curses.

Deuteronomy 30:15, 19 says, "See I have set before you today life and good, death and evil . . . therefore choose life . . ." You have a choice—blessings or curses.

We chose that day to forgive and repent of all word curses that had been said out of the mouth of our ancestors. We asked God to forgive us and remove all the iniquities that had come upon us due to those depression years when great lack was throughout the United States. That proved to be one of the great turning points in our lives.

Familiar Spirits

Now, let's look at familiar spirits. Why are they familiar? These spirits are familiar with our bloodline, or our generation. They follow us, generation after generation until they feel right at home, or familiar, in their "house."

Jesus taught:

> When an unclean spirit goes out of a man, he goes through dry places, seeking rest, and finds none. Then he says, "I will return to my house from which I came." And when he comes he finds it empty, swept, and put in order.
>
> —Matthew 12:43–44

That word *house* that is used in the Greek can also be interpreted "generation." So the spirit returns to the familiar generation from which it came.

23

> "Then he goes and takes with him seven other
> spirits more wicked than himself, and they enter
> and dwell there; and the last state of that man is
> worse than the first. So shall it also be with this
> wicked generation."
>
> —MATTHEW 12:45

The number of spirits gathered together is significant.
The one spirit gathers seven other spirits to come with
him to make a total of eight spirits. The number seven
signifies completion, so naturally the number eight signifies a new beginning. In other words, the demon gathers
seven others in order to create a new beginning that will
destroy you.

I also believe that when the wicked spirit gets other
spirits more wicked than he, these spirits are not only
more wicked, but also stronger. The longer an iniquity
stays in a family, the worse it becomes and the harder it is
to dislodge. The good part is that He is a covenant-
keeping God as we are told in Psalm 105:8: "He
remembers His covenant forever, the Word which He
commanded, for a thousand generations."

JACOB'S FAMILY

Let's follow a family weakness and see the consequences of their decision to "do it their way and not
God's way." Their way was lying, cheating, manipu-
lating, deceiving, favoritism and control.

> Now it came to pass, when Isaac was old and his
> eyes were so dim that he could not see, that he
> called Esau his older son and said to him, "My
> son." And he answered him, "Here I am." Then he
> said, "Behold now, I am old. I do not know the day

24

of my death. Now therefore, please take your weapons, your quiver and your bow, and go out to the field and hunt game for me. And make me savory food, such as I love, and bring it to me that I may eat, that my soul may bless you before I die."

—GENESIS 27:1–4

The custom of the Jewish patriots was to bless the eldest son before they died. Jacob actually asked Esau to prepare a covenant meal for the two of them to make a blood covenant so the blessings could be passed on to Esau and all his offspring. The father's blessing that would be spoken to his son at this ceremony said, "Be exalted, be lifted up, be reproductive in every area of your life, prosperous, victorious and having God's favor."

Isaac's wife, Rebekah, overheard the conversation. She had always petted Jacob and favored him over Esau. After Esau went to the open country to hunt for game that he might bring it back to his father, Rebekah said to Jacob, her younger son,

> "See here, I heard your father say to Esau, your brother, bring me some game, and make me appetizing meat, so that I may eat, and declare my blessing upon you before the LORD before my death. Now therefore, my son, obey my voice according to what I command you. Go now to the flock and bring me from there two choice kids of the goats, and I will make savory food from them for your father, such as he loves. Then you shall take it to your father, that he may eat it, and that he may bless you before his death."
>
> —GENESIS 27:6–10

Rebekah taught her son to lie, cheat, steal and deceive.

Through lying, deception and scheming, the two of them planned to deceive Isaac and cheat Esau out of his blessing. Rebekah even designed new clothing for Jacob and became a makeup artist to change his appearance. Jacob was smooth and Esau was hairy. Rebekah did not let a little thing like that stop her. She had Jacob steal Esau's clothing and wear them, and then she had him bring her the goat hair so she could put the skins of the kids of the goats on his hands and on the smooth part of his neck.

Jacob said to his mother: "Perhaps my father will feel me, and I shall seem to be a deceiver to him; and I shall bring a curse on myself and not a blessing" (v. 12). But his mother said to him, "Let your curse be on me, my son; only obey my voice, and go, get them for me" (v. 13).

At this point she put a word curse on herself. Rebekah and Jacob managed to deceive Isaac and because of this Jacob received Esau's blessing. When Esau discovered that his blessing had been stolen, he was filled with hate toward his brother. He threatened to kill him.

Now, Mama cannot have her favorite son getting killed, so she manipulates and dominates a bit more and suggests that Jacob flee to her brother Laban in Haran. She manages to convince Isaac to send him on his way by telling him that she is weary of her life and does not want to live if Jacob takes a wife of the daughters of the Hittite. (Notice how she puts the curse of death on herself). Isaac called Jacob and blessed him and commanded him, "You shall not marry one of the women of Canaan."

As a result of losing his blessing, Esau now hated his brother, had murder in his heart, and was rebellious toward his parents. He married a Canaanite woman just to spite his parents.

Let's follow the curses brought about by a mother not "training up a child in the way it should go" (Prov. 22:6).

1. **Humiliation.** Esau's marriage to a heathen woman dishonored and humiliated his parents.

2. **Mental and physical sickness.** Rebekah became so depressed and mentally confused that she said she wanted to die.

3. **Family breakdown.** Esau hated his brother, rebelled against his parents, and Jacob had to leave home.

4. **Poverty.** Jacob had to get out of his father's house and go to work for his uncle, who cheated him, used him and lied. What we sow we reap. Be careful what you plant in the garden of your heart. It will grow a crop and you will have to eat the fruit thereof.

5. **Disfavor.** He worked hard for seven years to earn Rachel for his bride and was cheated out of his first love.

6. **Oppression.** Can you image thinking you are married to the girl that you love and waking up with her older sister, Leah, whose eyes were weak and dull looking? Rachel was beautiful and very young and attractive. Talk about depression . . .

7. **Failure.** At this point in time, any of the events in Jacob's life would make him feel like a failure.

8. **God's disfavor.** Jacob brought this on himself when he lied to his father and agreed to go along with his mother's scheme to deceive his brother and father.

9. **Barrenness.** Jacob's first wife, Leah, had many babies, but his second wife, Rachel, remained barren for many years. But, after much prayer and many children birthed from her maids, God took pity on her. After she wrestled in prayer, she conceived and bore Jacob a son named Joseph.

10. **Self-imposed curse.** Rebekah said to her son, Jacob, "Go and get the blessing from your father Isaac." Jacob responded, "Maybe father

will discover I am a deceiver and curse me instead of bless me." Rebekah replied, "Upon me be thy curse, my son." She pronounced a curse upon herself. Read the entire story and you will find that Rebekah never again saw her son, Jacob. She was dead by the time he returned from Haran. We find that Rebekah began using language like, "I am weary of my life, because of the daughters of Heth [daughters of the land]. What good will my life be to me?" (Gen. 27:46). This is typical language of a person under a curse.

Rachel and Jacob decided to outwit Laban, and while he was away shearing his sheep they left and Rachel took the household gods. Laban returned home and found them gone and pursued them. After many days he caught up with them. He wanted to know who had stolen his household gods. Jacob, not knowing that Rachel had stolen them, said to Laban, "With whomever you find your gods, do not let him live" (Gen. 31:32). Jacob, in all innocence, put a word curse on his beloved wife. With his mouth he sentenced her to death. The next time Rachel gave birth, which was not much later, she died in childbirth (Gen. 35:18). This is cause and effect. She took the forbidden god into her household. Joseph put a word curse on her and sentenced her to die.

TAKE AUTHORITY

If you are suffering under the torment of a curse, somehow it found an opening. Do not get caught up with defending yourself. In the light of what you have just read, look at the incidents in your life that you just thought were coincidences. Ask God, From where did the curse come? Was it manipulation, domination, lying, cheating, stealing? Remember, curses go to the fourth generation and the blessings to the thousandth generation. Recognizing there is a curse and taking responsibility regardless of the cause is the beginning of freedom. We, as people, like to make excuses and blame someone else. Where there's sin, there's a curse, and God just wants us to repent.

By repenting of your sins you release yourself in the name of Jesus. We are cleansed of *all* sins by applying the blood of Jesus. Resisting the devil and renouncing his authority over you removes his legal right to operate in your life. Also, make sure you loose yourself of any bitterness or unforgiveness in your heart. (Later in this book there will be several chapters on how to forgive.) Take your rightful authority over the curse in the name of Jesus and rebuke it.

··

CHAPTER 3

The Facts About Evil Powers

I grew up in a Spirit-filled home, so one would think that the occult would not have been practiced in the household. I never remember being taught about the occult, horoscope, or witches when I was a young girl. If the subject ever came up I have no memory of ever hearing about the counterfeit of God's gifts. Yet we participated regularly in what is called superstition. For example, I was taught: "Don't walk under a ladder, and don't let a black cat cross the road in front of you—either of these would bring bad luck. If you are walking with someone and they go on one side of the pole and you on the other, immediately say 'bread and butter,' otherwise you will have a fight. The number thirteen was considered unlucky."

After a chicken dinner, we did a special thing with the "pulley-bone" (or wishbone) from the chicken breast. After dinner whoever had the pulley-bone would hold it and another family member would pull on it. Whoever got the long end (that was the hard one to get) would place the pulley-bone over the door and make a wish. As a girl, I can remember wishing the person that I was going to marry would walk under the wishbone. Often the next person to walk through the door would be a neighbor who was not available or even a possibility. This would bring about a lot of laughter and kidding. So these were considered good things to do because they brought laughter into the home.

The devil is a deceiver, and he encourages people to have fun in sin. If there were no pleasure when one first gets involved in superstition, then no one would do it. The devil is good at setting traps for the innocent. Even though I was reared by two very godly parents, these things were not considered evil. They were just considered family folklore and practiced by our family and by our neighbors. However, the things we were doing in the name of superstition were rooted in the occult practices.

Superstition originates in the occult and witchcraft. It is not just a funny game. These so-called games were doors that opened my soulish nature to be curious and seek more power. In later years I turned from the faith that I was raised in to seek answers in the occult. The Word says, "Train up a child in the way he should go, and when he is old he will not depart from it" (Prov. 22:6). As a young girl I attended Sunday school, memorized scriptures and carried my Bible to church each Sunday. One can do all these things and still not have their eyes opened. The devil's job is to steal, kill and destroy. He can best do this when one is ignorant of his devices. The occult is his territory.

I saw many people healed when I was a teenager. I remember when an evangelist came to my hometown during the polio epidemic. Over a six-week-long healing revival I saw fifty to sixty people per night healed from the crippling disease of polio, throw their crutches away and walk normally. Some who were in wheelchairs got up and walked; tumors disappeared from bodies; eyes of the blind opened; the deaf were healed. But even seeing all these miracles did not keep me on the straight and narrow.

I have always had a great curiosity about the supernatural. The problem was I just chose to do it the wrong way earlier in my life. There is enough power in the name of Jesus to quench all my curiosity. I only needed to appropriate it.

I remember one superstition that I participated in as a child, and it made a lasting impression on me. I had a wart on my heel. This was very uncomfortable and hurt when my shoe would rub it. I was told by an aunt to take the rag that Mother used to clean her wood stove with and not let anyone know that I was taking it. I was to rub the rag on the wart and then bury it. I did as instructed, and the next morning the wart was gone. I remember Mother asking if anyone had seen the rag that she used to clean the cook stove. I kept very quiet. Finally, I was asked directly if I had seen her rag. I lied and told her no. The word *occult* means "to cover up, to hide." I felt guilty for lying to my mother. But, I wanted to hide what I had done in order to keep the healing that had occurred through the lie and deception of the enemy.

As an adult, when I was faced with overwhelming pressures of life, I again sought solutions from illegitimate power. I became most deeply involved in occult practices when my first marriage ended in divorce—after two children and nine years of trying. Instead of turning to the church, I turned to studying Jean Dixon, reading my horoscope daily for direction, following Edgar Cayce's teachings for healing and consulting mediums. The Ouija board was my answer for direction, and I believed in reincarnation. As you can see, I was looking for answers but in all the wrong places. I was literally being taken captive by the devil because of ignorance of the Word.

I had felt just enough power through what we called superstition that I thought this was a more powerful way than depending on God. I convinced myself that religion was old-fashioned and out of date. But even then I still attended church just enough to appease my conscience, and when Mother asked where I was attending church I could at least tell her a name of a church.

SATAN'S FALL

Let's look at Deuteronomy 18: 9–14.

> When you come into the land which the LORD your God is giving you, you shall not learn to follow the abominations of those nations. *There shall not be found among you anyone who makes his son or his daughter pass through the fire*, or one who practices witchcraft, or a soothsayer, or one who interprets omens, or a sorcerer, or one who conjures spells, or a medium, or a spiritist, or one who called up the dead. For all who do these things are an abomination to the LORD, and because of these abominations the LORD your God drives them out from before you. You shall be blameless before the LORD your God. For these nations which you will dispossess listened to soothsayers and diviners; but as for you, the LORD your God has not appointed such for you (italics added).

Let's look specifically at God's commandment not to make a son or daughter pass through the fire. Why is it a sin to pass through the fire? I think the answer goes back to the time when Satan (originally called Lucifer) was the worship leader of the Pre-Adamic Age. God described him this way: "You were the anointed cherub who covers; I established you; You were on the holy mountain of God; *You walked back and forth in the midst of fiery stones.* You were perfect in your ways from the day you were created, Till *iniquity* was found in you" (Ezek. 28:14–15, italics added). Why did Lucifer walk up and down in the midst of the stones of fire? I believe the stones represent the cleansing fire of God. As Lucifer the anointed cherub would walk on the coals of fire, the glory of the Lord would rise upon him. When he was full of glory out of the overflow of the presence of God, he would lead praise and worship. As He led praise and worship a great cloud of glory would come up out of him because of the fire of God.

Because of pride Lucifer fell and became Satan. Now he wants people to walk on coals of fire to bring worship and honor to his name. In order to walk on coals of fire, a person has to meditate. One must meditate until they are in a trance-like state of mind so the coals will not burn them. Meditation of this type comes from the soulish nature, which is the mind, will and emotions.

The Word of God tells us that we are kept in perfect peace when our minds are stayed on God. But when our minds are given over to evil spirits we lose our peace. Our soulish nature is then empowered by the devil and therefore pays honor to him. He desires to be worshiped, but God is the only one we are to worship.

The second thing I want to discuss about Lucifer's fall is the cause. Ezekiel said that "iniquity" was found in him. Isaiah explains what was this iniquity.

> How you are fallen from heaven, O Lucifer, son of
>   the morning!
> How you are cut down to the ground, you who

weakened the nations!
For you have said in your heart,
'I WILL ascend into heaven,
I WILL exalt my throne above the stars of God;
I WILL also sit on the mount of the congregation
    on the farthest sides of the north;
I WILL ascend above the heights of the clouds,
I WILL be like the Most High.'

—ISAIAH 14:12–14

Satan fell because of pride. He wanted to be God. There are five "I will's" in Lucifer's declaration, so Satan has a fivefold army to destroy the church. From the foundation of the earth, God established a fivefold ministry to build up the church. Satan never had an original idea. Everything he does is a counterfeit to God's laws, which are made to protect us and bring good into our lives. Satan fell because he became prideful and decided that he was so good, that everyone should worship him instead of God. All the occult practices mentioned in Deuteronomy 18 were used as tools of worship in opposition to the good that God has established. Satan wants to be worshiped as God is worshiped.

SATAN'S STRATEGIC FORCES

In order to effectively neutralize Satan and his forces, we need to understand how and where they operate.

Satan makes his dwelling place in the second heavens. What we see with our physical eye is the stellar heavens, and where Satan lives is the second heavens where principalities, powers and the rulers of the darkness of this age, spiritual hosts of wickedness in the heavenly places abide with him (Eph. 6:12).

Scripture indicates that the earth is the home for the demonic forces called demons or evil spirits. We read in

Matthew 12:43–44: "When an unclean spirit goes out of a man, he goes through dry places, seeking rest, and finds none. Then he says, 'I will return to my house from which I came.' And when he comes, he finds it empty, swept, and put in order."

When it says he 'passes through' dry places does not refer to him ascending or descending. So from this it appears that the demons movement is here on earth. The ones on earth are assigned to us through the bloodline iniquities in our families. Their job is to see that the plan of God for our lives is thwarted.

Scripture gives us some insight into the origination of the earth-bound demons. First, let's look at the creation account. In Genesis 1:1 it says that God created the heavens and the earth. In Genesis 1:2 it says the earth was without form and void and darkness covered it. Everything that God creates is good, so I do not believe He originally created the earth as a dark, formless void. I believe the original earth was beautiful and full of plants, animals, and, people. Its downfall came when Satan was cast out of heaven and fell down to earth. People on earth followed him and became unredeemed and evil. Because of Satan, all of creation fell into chaos, and the spirits of the people came under Satan's rule. These spirits remained on earth, and when God repopulated the earth, they set about to find human beings to enter so they could express themselves. Demons inhabit people who are involved in the occult.

If you have ever spent much time in intercessory prayer you have wrestled with Satan's forces. The Word of God tells us that we pull down those strongholds and stop their attacks. Following is a description of the forces we are called to defeat.

1. Earth-bound demons. These are at the very bottom of the hierarchy, and they follow the commands of others.

2. Principalities. These are privates in Satan's army—common fallen angels who come against ordinary people, especially Christians. I believe these are sergeants over the earth-bound demons. They are familiar with our bloodline iniquities and their assignment is to attack, harass and torment.

3. Powers. The powers (or authorities) derive their power from and execute the will of the chief rulers. These are fallen angels who have even greater authority and power than principalities. They assign earth-bound demons to oppress people who are in positions of leadership in businesses, schools or churches.

4. Rulers of darkness. They could also be called world-rulers of the darkness of this age, or the spirit-world rulers. These fallen angels are assigned to oppress and attack cities.

5. Spiritual wickedness in high places. This describes fallen angels who are the generals in Satan's army. They steer national leaders and countries toward drugs, pornography, alcoholism, all kinds of evil and wickedness that controls, oppresses and possesses national leaders.

6. Satan. He is at the top. When he fell he took one third of the angels with him. He is ruler of all fallen angels and demons. Notice I said ruler. In other words, he has the rulership over them But, he is not the final authority. When Jesus died on the cross he took the keys to death, hell, and the grave. Colossians 2:10 tells us who is ultimately in control: "And you are complete in Him, who is the *head of all principalities and power*" (italics added).

Ephesians. 1:20–23 also states: "Which He worked in Christ when He raised Him from the dead and seated him at His right hand in the heavenly places, far above all principality and power and might and dominion, and every name that is named, not only in this age but also in that which is to come. And He put all things under His feet, and gave Him to be head over all things in the church, which is His body, the fullness of Him who fills all in all."

OCCULT PRACTICES

We have discussed that occult practices open the door for demonic activity in our lives. Many people are not aware of what are occult practices, for they are so common that they are often accepted as a part of culture. Here are some of the practices we commonly hear about, along with how they are defined in Webster's dictionary.

Witchcraft. The practice or art of witches; sorcery; enchantments; intercourse with evil spirits.

Sorcery. The power of magic, or especially of divination, gained by the assistance or control of evil spirits.

Divination. To foresee or foretell. The act or practice of foreseeing the future or of discovering hidden knowledge, as by study of omens.

Necromancy. The art of claiming to foretell the future by alleged communication with the dead; black magic.

Occult sciences. Sciences that relate to the supposed action of influence of occult qualities, or supernatural powers, as alchemy (the art of extracting medicinal juices from plants) magic, necromancy and astrology.

Alchemy. Often associated with medieval folklore, this is a chemical science and speculative philosophy designed to transform base metals into gold. It is figuratively used regarding the change of base human nature into the divine. In other words, by drinking the "golden" formula you will be changed into a god.

Astrology or Horoscope. A so-called science that relies on the influence of the stars upon human events and on the foretelling of events by means of the stars. Horoscope is the situation of planets or stars with respect to each other at a given time. A chart or map showing the relative positions of the stars, used by astrologers in making predictions.

Soothsayer. A person who foretells events.

Charmer. Any action, speech or object believed to have magic power; a spell; talisman. An object worn to keep one from harm or to bring good fortune; an amulet; hence, a small ornament, such as a seal, worn on a watch chain or a locket. A trait or quality that fascinates or allures, as if by a spell.

How often do you see someone with a charm bracelet? On it there is a four-leaf clover, which stands for good luck. The Italian horn that is worn around the neck is a good luck charm that is supposed to bring prosperity. Many people hang a horseshoe upside down over their door for good luck. Some carry a rabbit's foot or a buckeye in their pocket for good luck. All this is connected to the Charmer. The amulet is an object worn to avert evil. A charm can also be a combination of words denoting magical powers of protection.

Anything that is used to foretell and guide like tea-leaf reader, palm reader, fortune telling are an abomination to God. How many of our public school and some private schools have school carnivals and set up palm readers and fortune-telling booths, thinking it is just an innocent game that will earn money for the school? How many of these children were just like me . . . a Christian, yet doing this and never being told it was wrong? Some of them become casualties and never become a Christian.

FEARS

I was a very fearful person when growing up. As I reflect on the radio programs that we listened to and the stories that we heard; I know exactly where that spirit of fear came in. Fear comes from hearing scary stories. We would listen to "The Squeaking Door," on radio and then I would have horrible nightmares. I used to walk in my sleep, to the point that it was dangerous. The old farm house that we lived in had a very high front porch. One night I woke up just as I started to walk off the porch. Another time I was standing up in the window casing and put my foot through the window and broke the glass, cutting my foot.

Bloody Mary is a teen-seance "game" in which participants spin around three times saying Bloody Mary, in a dark room, such as a bathroom, with their eyes tightly shut, then open them suddenly, and look into a mirror for a scary face to appear. My granddaughter did this and saw a skeleton in the mirror with long blonde hair and piercing black eyes but the rest of the creature was just bones with a beautiful flowing white dress. It scared her so badly that she confessed to her mother what she had done. She repented of having been involved in the occult. Then she commanded the spirit of fear to leave her body and she stopped having nightmares about her one-time experience of playing Bloody Mary.

Fear torments. While attending a birthday party, my daughter who was in the seventh grade at that time, was part of levitating a table. She knew this was wrong. But, went along with the crowd. Not long after that she and I were driving by a Spiritualist Church that was located in Dover Shores at the time. I felt this cold presence enter my car. I looked at my daughter and she was absolutely panic stricken and having trouble breathing. I immediately began pleading the blood of Jesus and, as I did, this "cold spirit and very evil feeling presence" left my car. I then began to question her and she told me what had happened at the party. She repented. The spirit they contacted that night to levitate the table had a legal right to attack her. Had she been by herself or with an unbeliever, that evil spirit would have entered her and attached itself to her and continued to torment, harass and eventually it would have destroyed her.

CONSULTING MEDIUMS

Medium: In spiritualism, a person is supposed to be able to transmit information from spirits or to do things impossible without their aid. I visited a medium one time (many years ago, before I was saved) and this is the way she "read" me. She asked for a piece of my jewelry that I was wearing. She took the necklace in her hand and ran her fingers around and around the black pearl necklace. I was sitting in a very comfortable chair facing her. The room was very pretty, there was a slight breeze and sheer curtains were blowing ever so gently. She began to tell me my grandfather and grandmother's name and described the lay of land that they lived on. At this time all she knew about me was my name. She was very accurate on some of her information and totally wrong on two very important things. She seemed to be a lot more accurate on what had already happened in my life and totally inaccurate on the future.

I paid her five dollars and as I started to leave she asked me to attend a Sunday night seance. I told her that I already had a religion and did not need to come back. She emphasized that I was easy to read and that I would fit in very nicely in their community. At this point I remember feeling fear, confusion, guilt and just deep down terror. I knew that what she had said and done was not from God. I knew that behind what she was saying was an evil spirit. At this time, I was not even sure what an evil spirit was, but I knew I was in the wrong place.

DEMONS AND THEIR EFFECTS

I would like to list for you the most common listings of demons and their groupings. This is not the list to end all lists but it does include most of the ones we have encountered through the years. They are listed in grouping, where we usually encounter them. I am listing them in alphabetical order and you will find there are over 53, at least one for every week of the year:

1. ACCUSATION: Criticism, Faultfinding, Judging.
2. ADDICTIVE AND COMPULSIVE: Alcohol, Caffeine, Drugs, Gluttony, Medications, Nicotine.
3. AFFECTATION: Play-acting, Pretension, Sophistication, Theatrics.
4. BITTERNESS: Anger, Hatred, Murder, Resentment, Retaliation, Temper, Unforgiveness, Violence.
5. COMPETITION: Argument, Driving, Ego, Pride.
6. CONFUSION: Forgetfulness, Frustration, Incoherence, Procrastination.
7. CONTROL: Anger, Argument, Dominance, Possessiveness, Witchcraft.
8. COVETOUSNESS: Discontent, Greed, Kleptomania, Material Lust, Stealing.
9. CULTS: Bahaism, Christian Science, Jehovah's Witnesses, Latihan, Lodges, societies, social agencies, using the Bible and God as a basis but omitting the blood atonement of Jesus, Mormonism, Rosicrucianism, Subud, Theosophy, Unitarianism, Unity, Urania.
10. CURSING: Backbiting, Belittling, Blasphemy,

Coarse jesting, Criticism, Gossip, Mockery, Railing.
11. DEATH: Abuse, Murder, Suicide.
12. DEPRESSION: Death, Defeatism, Dejection, Despair, Despondency, Discouragement, Hopelessness, Insomnia, Morbidity, Suicide.
13. DOUBT: Intellectionism, Skepticism, Unbelief.
14 ESCAPE: Alcohol, Drugs, Indifference, Passivity, Sleepiness, Stoicism.
15. FALSE BURDENS: False Responsibility, False Compassion.
16. FALSE RELIGIONS: Buddhism, Confucianism, Hinduism, Islam Shintoism, Taoism.
17. FATIGUE: Laziness, Tiredness, Weariness.
18. FEAR OF AUTHORITY: Deceit, Lying, Manipulation.
19. FEARS (ALL KINDS): Hysteria, Phobias.
20. GLUTTONY: Compulsive eating, Frustration, Idleness, Nervousness, Resentment, Self-pity, Self-reward.
21. GRIEF: Cruel, Crying, Heartache, Heartbreak, Sadness, Sorrow.
22. GUILT: Condemnation, Embarrassment, Shame, Unworthiness.
23. HEAVINESS. Burden, Disgust, Gloom.
24. HYPERACTIVITY: Driving, Pressure, Restlessness.
25. IMPATIENCE: Agitation, Criticism, Frustration, Intolerance, Resentment.
26. INDECISION: Compromise, Confusion, Forgetfulness, Indifference, Procrastination.
27. INFIRMITY: Could be any disease, regardless of name.
28. INHERITANCE: Curses, Emotional, Mental, Physical.
29. INSECURITY: Inadequacy, Ineptness, Inferiority, Loneliness, Self-pity, Shyness, Timidity.
30. JEALOUSY: Distrust, Envy, Selfish, Suspicion.

31. MENTAL ILLNESS: Hallucinations, Insanity, Madness, Mania, Paranoia, Retardation, Schizophrenia, Senility.

32. MIND-BINDING: Confusion, Fear of Failure, Fear of Man, Occult spirits, Spiritism spirits.

33. MIND IDOLATRY: Ego, Intellectualism, Pride, Rationalization.

34. NERVOUSNESS: Excitement, Headache, Insomnia, Nervous habits, Restlessness, Roving, Tension.

35. OCCULT: Astrology, Automatic Handwriting, Black magic, Charms Fetishes, etc., Conjugation Incantation, ESP, Fortune-telling, Handwriting Analysis, Horoscope, Hypnotism, Levitation, Ouija Board, Palmistry, Pendulum, Tarot Cards, Water Witching, White Magic, Witchcraft.

36. PARANOIA: Distrust, Envy, Fears, Jealousy, Persecution, Fears, Suspicion.

37. PASSIVITY: Funk, Indifference, Lethargy, Listlessness.

38. PERFECTION: Anger, Ego, Criticism, Frustration, Intolerance, Irritability, Pride, Vanity.

39. PERSECUTION: Fear of Accusation, Fear of Condemnation. Fear of Judgment, Fear of Reproof, Sensitiveness, Unfairness.

40. PRIDE: Arrogance, Ego, Haughtiness, Importance, Self-righteousness, Vanity.

41. REBELLION: Anti-submissiveness, Disobedience, Self-will, Stubbornness, Witchcraft.

42. REJECTION: Fear of rejection, Self-rejection.

43. RELIGIOUS: Destruction, Doctrinal Error, Doctrinal Obsession, Fear of God, Fear of Hell, Fear of Lost Salvation, Formalism, Legalism, Religiosity, Ritualism.

44. RETALIATION: Cruelty, Destruction, Hatred, Hurt, Spite, Sadism. / Revenge —

45. SCHIZOPHRENIA: Manic-depressive, Bi-Polar.

46. SELF-ACCUSATION: Self-condemnation, Self-hatred.
47. SELF-DECEPTION: Pride, Self-delusion, Self-seduction.
48. SENSITIVENESS: Fear of Disapproval, Fear of Man, Self-awareness.
49. SEXUAL IMPURITY: Adultery, Exposure, Fantasy Lust, Fornication, Frigidity, Harlotry, Homosexuality, Incest, Lesbianism, Lust, Masturbation, Rape.
50. SPIRITISM: Necromancy, Seance, Spirit guide.
51. STRIFE: Argument, Bickering, Contention, Fighting, Quarreling.
52. WITHDRAWAL: Daydreaming, Fantasy, Pouting, Pretension, Unreality.
53. WORRY: Anxiety, Apprehension, Dread, Fear.

I am sure there are more demons that we have not listed. The Bible says that Hell enlarges itself and it is possible that demons also are being loosed in these last days that we have not encountered before.

To free yourself from the demons use your will. Take authority over them by calling the demon by their name and command them to leave your body. They came in with a breath they can leave with a breath. As you speak by the authority of God's Word with your mouth they will leave. If you have any I.O.U.'s against anybody tear them up and leave that person in the hands of God. Renounce the occult. Confess sin as sin. Repentance means turning away from evil and embracing the knowledge of God.

After you have taken these steps to free yourself. Avoid idols, stop any forbidden practices and get rid of any occult objects that you have in your home. Burn any books or objects that represent any of the forbidden practices.

To stay free daily read your Bible. Both faith and unbelief come from what we read. What you put in your heart will be spoken with your mouth. "The tongue has the power of life and death" (Prov. 18:21). Pray first thing in the morning. When you say the Lord's prayer you say . . ."deliver us from evil and lead us not into temptation" (Matt. 6:13). You are at that time praying a hedge of protection around yourself. Plead the blood of Jesus over yourself, possession, family, school, work and pets.

Stay filled with the Holy Ghost. Avoid situations, people, places or things that cause you to sin. Avoid complaining, and develop an attitude of gratitude.

CHAPTER 4

Sources of Generational Curses

Many years ago my husband researched the genealogy of both his family and my family. To our surprise, we found that both of our families had many preachers in past generations. Neither of us had known anything about our families beyond our great-grandparents. What a blessing it was to discover a godly heritage.

At the end of this chapter you will find a drawing of a family tree. Use this as a guide to determine whether any roots of generational curses are operative in your life. As my husband and I researched our family background we discovered roots that we had not previously uncovered.

Does iniquity takes dominion over a family tree? Psalm 119:133 says, "Direct my steps by Your word, and let no iniquity have dominion over me." Because of iniquity the love of many wax cold (Matt. 24:12). If iniquity in a family isn't removed, then the family is cold toward God because iniquities have never been cleansed and

47

they separate us from God. Iniquity can even take dominion over a nation.

> "We have sinned and committed iniquity, we have done wickedly and rebelled, even by departing from Your precepts and Your judgments. Neither have we heeded Your servants the prophets, who spoke in Your name to our kings and our princes, to our fathers and all the people of the land. O Lord, righteousness belongs to You, but to us shame of face, as it is this day—to the men of Judah, to the inhabitants of Jerusalem and all Israel, those near and those far off in all the countries to which You have driven them, because of the unfaithfulness which they have committed against You.
>
> O Lord, to us belongs shame of face, to our kings, our princes, and our fathers, because we have sinned against You. To the Lord our God belong mercy and forgiveness, though we have rebelled against Him. We have not obeyed the voice of the Lord our God, to walk in His laws, which He set before us by His servants the prophets. Yes, all Israel has transgressed Your law, and has departed so as not to obey Your voice; therefore the curse and the oath written in the Law of Moses the servant of God have been poured out on us, because we have sinned against Him. And He has confirmed His words, which He spoke against us and against our judges who judged us, by bringing upon us a great disaster; for under the whole heaven such has never been done as what has been done to Jerusalem."
>
> —DANIEL 9:5–12

But how can we pass from curses to blessing? We are told in Galatians that Christ has redeemed us from the curse so the "the blessing of Abraham might come upon the Gentiles in Christ Jesus" (Gal. 3:13–14). Iniquity can be cleansed through a prayer of repentance.

It is so easy to be set free by Jesus because He paid the price of iniquity for us. (See Isaiah 53:5.)

We are told in Hosea 4:6: "My people are destroyed for lack of knowledge. Because you have rejected knowledge, I also will reject you from being priest for Me; Because you have forgotten the law of your God, I also will forget your children." Since we now have the knowledge, we can turn the curse into a blessing. The reverse of this scripture can become a reality in our lives: "Because we have not forgotten the law of our God, He also will not forget our children!" We need to make a decision to get set free of all iniquities.

IDENTIFYING INIQUITIES

Remember, the Bible says a curse does not come without a cause. To help you look for root causes in your family tree, I have listed twelve of the most common iniquities that cause curses.

1. Idolatry, false gods, the occult. This the key root to identify first, for God commanded: "You shall not make for yourself a carved image — any likeness of anything that is in heaven above, or that is in the earth beneath, or that is in the water under the earth; you shall not bow down to them nor serve them. For I, the Lord your God, am a jealous God, visiting the iniquity of the fathers upon the children to the third and fourth generations of those who hate Me" (Exod. 20:4–5).

2. Dishonoring parents. We are told in Ephesians 6:2–3: "'Honor your father and mother,' which is the first commandment with promise: 'that it may be well with you and you may live long on the earth.'" The "promise"

49

is a blessing, and the opposite of a blessing is a curse. The choice is ours.

3. Illicit or unnatural sex. Leviticus 20:10–21 lists these perversions, including adultery, fornication, incest, homosexuality, bestiality, and says they are an abomination! All who indulge in sexual perversion of any kind expose themselves to the curse of God.

4. Injustice to the weak or helpless. The Bible tells us in Exodus 23:7: "Keep yourself far from a false matter; do not kill the innocent and righteous. For I will not justify the wicked." The supreme example of that in our society today is deliberate abortion. Recognize the curse, repent of the sin of murder, and ask for God's mercy. Symbolically, take your baby in your arms, look it in the face and name the baby so that you can identify yourself as the parent. God will give you a name even if you don't know the gender. Say to the baby: "I ask you to forgive me for taking your earthly life away from you. I cannot bring you back, but I will join you someday." Now, lift the baby up in both hands and say, "I present you to Jesus." Finally, lay the baby in a basket, box, coffin, close the lid, put a bouquet of flowers on top, lower it into the ground. Taking these steps brings closure to what was done and gives the baby an identity. In so doing, you recognize that the fetus taken from your body was not a piece of tissue, but a baby. God's Word is very clear that each baby is uniquely made. (See Psalm 139:15–16, KJV.)

After this you will feel the guilt, shame, and heaviness leaving your body. You will be able to weep tears that will cleanse you from the defilement that came when you had the abortion. Quite frequently women are barren, or have many miscarriages, because of the guilt of having an abortion. When the guilt is dealt with, the female organs are often healed, and they are able to conceive and

50

carry the baby to full term. Some women who had abortions will go on to give birth to other children but they cannot really enjoy them because of the guilt and shame. After following the steps given for closure they have a greater love for their children and live a more peaceful life.

5. Trusting in the arm of flesh. This means thinking you don't need God, that you are quite sufficient within yourself. Some are so prideful and independent that they think it would be demeaning to their character to trust in God. This is the sin of pride, and pride goes before a fall (Prov. 16:18). Jeremiah 17:5–6 says: "Thus says the Lord: 'Cursed is the man who trusts in man and makes flesh his strength, whose heart departs from the Lord, for he shall be like a shrub in the desert, and shall not see when good comes, but shall inhabit the parched places in the wilderness, in a salt land which is not inhabited.'"

6. Stealing or perjury. This is part of the Ten Commandments and will invite a curse upon us if we break them. "You shall not steal. You shall not bear false witness against your neighbor" (Deut. 5:19–20).

7. Being financially stingy with God. "Bring all the tithes into the store house, that there may be food in My house, And try Me now in this," says the Lord of hosts, "if I will not open for you the windows of heaven and pour out for you such blessing that there will not be room enough to receive it. And I will rebuke the devourer for your sakes, so that he will not destroy the fruit of your ground, Nor shall the vine fail to bear fruit for you in the field, Says the Lord of hosts; And all the nations will call you blessed, for you will be a delightful land, Says the Lord of hosts" (Malachi 3:10–12). Malachi 1:14 speaks of the curse: "'But cursed be the deceiver who has in his flock a male, and takes a vow, but sacrifices to the Lord what is blemished — for I am a great King,' says the

Lord of hosts, 'and My name is to be feared among the nations.'"

8. Negative words spoken by persons with relational authority. These are words spoken by parents, husbands, teachers, pastors and so forth. Many times these words were simply meant to discourage people, but in reality they became a curse. A teacher may say, "That was a stupid answer," but the child receives it as meaning he is stupid and therefore a curse comes with the remark. Word curses are spoken by those in authority include: "You'll fail if you leave this company," or, "You'll fail if you leave this church." These things are curses regardless of the intent of the person pronouncing them. Psalm 36:3 says, "The words of his mouth are wickedness and deceit; he has ceased to be wise and to do good."

9. Self-imposed curses. These are curses that people pronounce upon themselves. (I will never amount to anything . . . I am just like my father or mother . . . and so on.)

10. Words pronounced by persons representing Satan, witch doctors, etc. The root sin behind Satan and those who practice witchcraft is rebellion. We know this for two reasons. First, Satan was cast out of heaven for rebellion. Second, the Bible says: "For rebellion is as the sin of witchcraft, and stubbornness is as iniquity and idolatry" (1 Sam. 15:23). In the original Hebrew, the word *as* was not there so this verse could be correctly translated as "For rebellion *is* the sin of witchcraft and stubbornness *is* iniquity and idolatry" (italics added). Any words pronounced by persons representing Satan in any way are of rebellion and therefore against God. Their curses can come upon us only if there is a chink in our armor. Remember, the Bible says "A curse causeless shall not alight" (Prov. 26:2).

11. Soulish prayers, utterances spoken in wrong attitudes and gossip. When a prayer is prayed against a *detailed plan, an focus* *flee from evil, bad company corrupts good morals.*

person, this is a soulish prayer. All our prayers should be to bless and not hurt. All our attitudes should be to lift up our brothers and sisters, not tear them down. Psalm 19:14 teaches us: "Let the words of my mouth and the meditation of my heart be acceptable in Your sight, O Lord, my Strength and my Redeemer."

12. Unscriptural covenants. It is unscriptural to be united by covenant with people who are aligned with forces that are evil and alien to God. Exodus 20:3 says "You shall have no others gods before me." When we unite ourselves with others that are not Christians, then we take on their gods, through that covenant. A specific example is involvement in Freemasonry or any like secret society.

HISTORICAL EXAMPLES OF CURSES

History records for us many instances of generational curses or cycles and the results of them. Jews have a self-imposed curse on their nation, for the Bible records that Pilate asked "Shall I let Him go?" (speaking of Jesus). The Jewish crowd said, "No, crucify Him!" Pilate said, "I'm innocent of the blood of this man." The Jewish crowd replied: His blood be on us and our children" (Matt. 27:25). Jacob's father, Isaac, proclaimed a blessing that, to this day, is God's protection against anti-semitism. "Let peoples serve you, And nations bow down to you. Be master over your brethren, And let your mother's sons bow down to you. Cursed be everyone who curses you, And blessed be those who bless you!" (Gen. 27:29).

Another true story involves two American families who have been traced through their generations.

Max Jukes was an atheist who married a godless woman. Some 560 descendants were traced:

310 died paupers
150 were criminals
7 were murdered
100 were known drunkards
More than half of the women were prostitutes

The descendants of Max Jukes cost the U.S. government more than $1.25 million in nineteenth century dollars.

Jonathan Edwards was a contemporary of Max Jukes. He was a committed Christian who gave God first place in his life. He married a godly lady, and some 1,394 descendants were traced:

295 graduated from college of whom 13 became college presidents and 65 became professors
3 were elected as U.S. senators
3 were elected as state governors
30 were judges
100 were lawyers (One was the dean of a medical school.)
75 became officers in the military
100 were well-known missionaries, preachers, and prominent authors
80 held some form of public office
3 were mayors of large cities
1 was comptroller of the U.S. Treasury
1 was vice president of the United States[1]

What a great difference there was in the offspring of these two men. When I first began to see the truth in breaking generational curses, I immediately thought about the influence it would have not only on me, but on my future offspring as well. I want to bless my children, grandchildren and future generations — not hand down generational curses. How about you?

1. Gibson, Noel & Phyl. *Evicting Demonic Squatters and Breaking Bondages.* (Freedom in Christ Ministries, 1987).

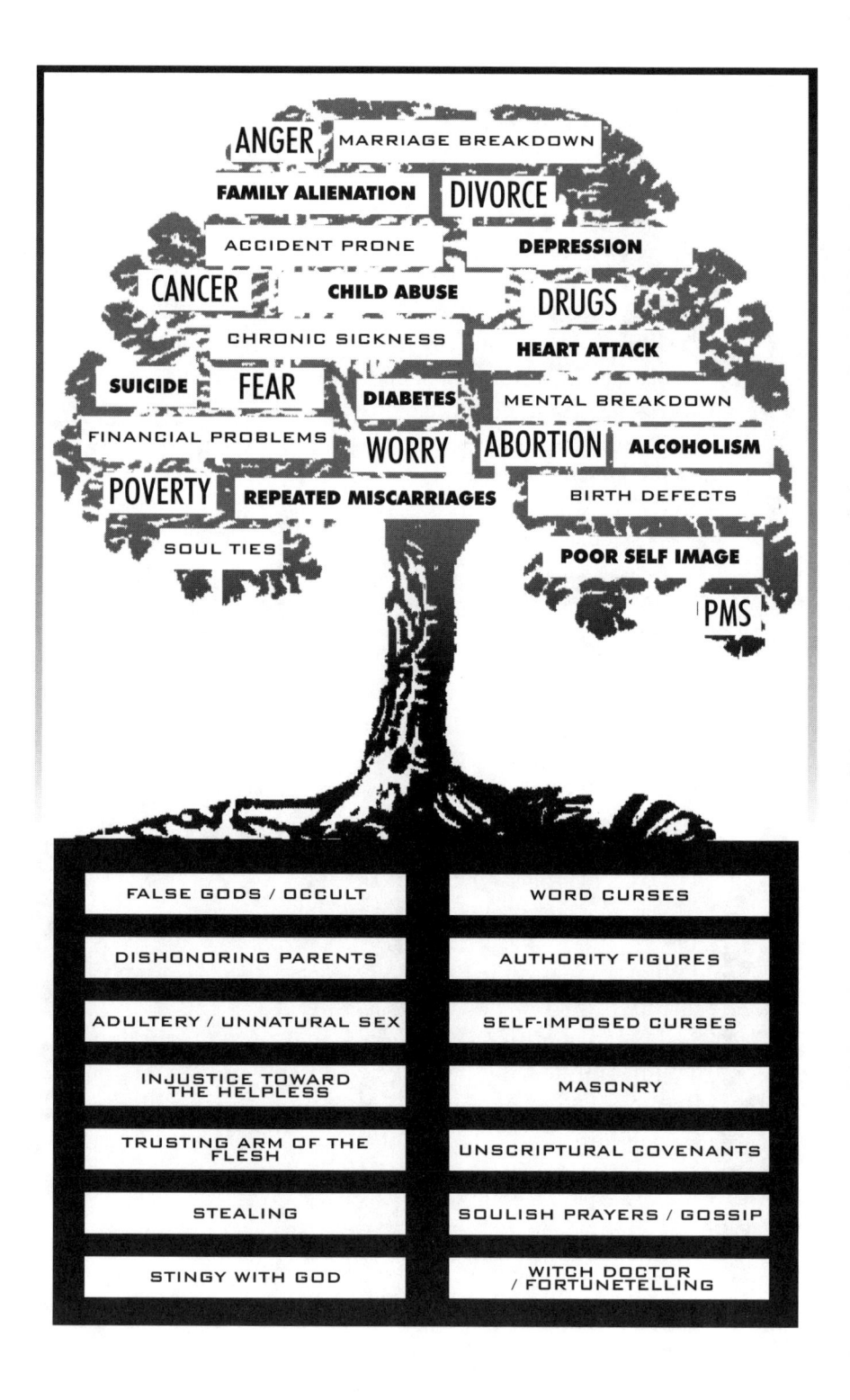

Part 2

....

Freed From the Curse

CHAPTER 5

··

Recognize the Problem

There are two attitudes that make it extremely difficult to get rid of a problem: 1) we do not know we have a problem, and 2) we refuse to admit we have a problem. We are all prideful, while some of us are more insistent than others that we do not have a problem.

Jeremiah 17:9 tells us, "The heart is deceitful above all things, and desperately wicked [or incurably sick]; who can know it?" We have to be aware of the fact that we could have iniquities operating in our lives and not be aware of them because of our deceitful hearts.

I think we must be ready to hear observations from other people or we will never be able to recognize problems in our own lives. Something about human nature will always make excuses to cover over the great needs in our lives. I call it self-deception. Proverbs 18:1 describes this attitude well: "A man who isolates himself seeks his own desire; he rages against all wise judgment."

When we find a truth in the Word we need to immediately assimilate it and see how we can make it work through Him. That's why Proverbs 18:10 encourages us to run to the Lord, "The name of the LORD is a strong tower; the righteous run to it and are safe."

Verses 14 and 15 continue: "The spirit of a man will sustain him in sickness, but who can bear a broken spirit? The heart of the prudent acquires knowledge, and the ear of the wise seeks knowledge." The final solution is to be set free and walk in freedom all our lives.

Hebrews 5:2 speaks of earthly priests, but it also points out a significant fact about people in general: "He can have compassion on those who are ignorant and going astray, since he himself is also subject to weakness." Did you understand the significance of this verse? It reveals two points: 1) we are ignorant of our problems, and 2) *because of this ignorance* we continue to go astray. It doesn't say we are stupid; it just says we are unaware of the problem. The answer is we must recognize the problem.

The definition of *recognize*, according to the dictionary is "to know because of having seen or met before." As we look at this definition, we know that we need some help from God and His Word because all things have been "seen or met before" by God. We need His knowledge so that we will recognize what we face.

CURSES ACQUIRED IN CHILDHOOD

Iniquities that come from our childhood are often suppressed by our minds. Both my husband and I have had many things come up as we talked over the things that happened in our childhoods. He grew up in western North Carolina in the Smoky Mountains and is the product of the culture that is prevalent there. I grew up in the foothills of the Ozarks in Arkansas and I am, of course, a product of the culture there. In our marriage, we talk to each other openly and we always have. Some husbands and wives talk very little but we are fortunate that, even when we were dating, we talked and shared with each other constantly. Due to this, we have recognized iniquities in each other and therefore told the other about the revelation.

My husband has always admitted to an iniquity of pride in his family. Due to the era he grew up in, there was more lack in the land than there was supply. About all there was to brag about was pride, so that was one of his family's strong points. He has always countered that with the scripture of Proverbs 11:2: "When pride comes, then comes shame; but with the humble is wisdom." Even today he strives to be humble so that God will reward him with wisdom.

Proverbs 16:18–19 says it well:

> Pride goes before destruction, and a haughty spirit before a fall. Better to be a humble spirit with the lowly, than to divide the spoil with the proud.

This iniquity had to be broken off him, as well as the iniquity of poverty.

My family was a study in different cultures.

My mother was born of a German father and a mother of English descent. Her father was a very dominant figure and freely stated his opinion. My mother was like that to some degree.

My father was born of an English father and a mother who was Cherokee Indian. He was somewhat like his mother—quite reserved and did not talk very much.

As you can imagine, the marriage between my mom and dad was quite a combination. Mom was always quite open and talked a lot. Dad was a hard one to figure out and never talked a lot. Still, they lived a fulfilled life, were married for more than sixty years, and raised five children.

In my own married life, I discovered iniquities in my own life that stemmed from these ancestors. Most obvious was the pride, probably rooted in my grandfather on my mother's side, being German, was quite prideful. I had always thought that it was a weakness to apologize and say, "I'm sorry," so I just never apologized. After we were married I learned just what I needed to do to break that iniquity off me. I was cooking supper, and my husband and two children were in what we called the "Florida room," watching a special television show they liked. I felt like I was not appreciated and was envious of the good time they seemed to be having.

At that point I could have made the decision to ask my husband to come and help me and he would have. But instead I decided to pitch myself a "pity party," and I stomped into the Florida room and informed all three of them I was not going to finish cooking supper. My husband looked up and said sympathetically, "You are all tired out. Go rest in your room, and I will finish cooking supper."

I slammed the door as I retreated to my room, and true to his word, he completed the supper without another word, fed the kids, helped them with their homework, and let them watch one more program before putting them to bed.

Meanwhile, I was finishing my pity party in my room by myself when the Lord instructed me to go out and apologize to my husband. It is really pathetic when you are more than thirty years of age and cannot remember ever telling anyone that you are sorry. When I got to the kitchen, there he stood in front of the sink, washing the dishes for me (because we did not have a dishwasher then) with tears in his eyes, because I just didn't feel good. At that point I would have had to look up to see the bottom of someone's foot. How low can you get?

That was my first time to honestly and completely apologize. That whole deal came about because of an iniquity. I recognized that iniquities that lurked in my life, and I took responsibility for them.

I hope you recognize any iniquities that may lurk in your life. Recognize them, repent of them, renounce them and prayed to be set free.

Curses That Hinder Marriages

We have discovered as we minister to married couples that many times their problems come from their childhood and from cultural differences. This was especially true some years ago when my husband and I were ministering in another state. Some of the church members were of another nationality and had been brought up in their culture and beliefs. Some of them had married into another nationality, whose culture was certainly not in line with their own. Problems arose, and we were faced with dealing with these situations.

One such couple we counseled (I will call them Bill and Jane) seemed to have more than their fair share of problems. Jane, who had been brought up in one culture, started dating Bill, who was reared in a different country. They fell in love and got married. Jane's father did not approve of Bill marrying his little girl, and that, in turn, caused more problems. Jane was a nominal Christian when they started dating, and Bill was not. After they married, many problems of misunderstanding erupted, some simply because of having to speak English to each other because their native languages were not the same.

Finally, after six or eight stormy years, Jane came to us

to see what could be done in their situation. We talked with Bill, and it seemed their differences were insurmountable. Still, with God all things are possible, so we encouraged him and told him that if he wanted his marriage to work he would have to get saved and change his life. The next Sunday at church he did just that and came forward and got gloriously saved. Praise God! A miracle had happened. We thought that would be the solution to the problems, but it was only the beginning.

Some of the zealots in the church (all sincere and well-meaning) tried to disciple him. They pointed out particular scriptures, such as Galatians 3:26–28:

> For you are all sons of God through faith in Christ Jesus. For as many of you as were baptized into Christ have put on Christ. There is neither Jew nor Greek, there is neither male nor female; for you are all one in Christ Jesus.

This scripture said there was no difference between male and female. This teaching was a shock to this man, because in his culture the man controlled the actions of the wife. This man's mentors had shown this scripture to him to get him to understand that his wife was also important in God's sight. However, the understanding he reached was that his culture was all wrong, so he decided to change things 180 degrees. Because of this, the pendulum swung too far in the opposite way.

Bill was a hard worker, and he worked in a nearby city, re-paving streets in the hot sun. He got his paycheck each week and never gave Jane any money until he got home and then only enough to get the bare necessities. The rest he spent as he pleased on whatever he pleased, as he had been accustomed to doing his entire life. Now, with this new scripture given to him, he knew he had been doing wrong, so he told Jane to meet him on a certain street where he would be working when he got his pay for the week. Of course, she was there, and he gave her the entire paycheck.

She was not accustomed to having that much money, and, just like a little child, she went shopping and bought all the things she had been wanting, regardless of whether she needed them or not. When he got home that night, they realized that neither of them had any money to go through the next week. Some kindly church people gave them some groceries, but again the next week the same scene was repeated. This had been going on for three weeks before I found out what was happening. I immediately called a meeting for the two of them, for they were at each other's throats.

"Why did you take all the money and spend it?" I asked Jane.

"He gave it to me," she pouted. "Besides he has been spending the money for years and I figured it was my chance to get even."

Jane also had grown up in a male-dominated culture, and she had never been given any money except a certain amount to buy a specific thing. Bill was trying to change, but he had no idea how to love someone and be a help-mate to them. They were both wrong, and yet, neither one was at fault because their problems stemmed from an iniquity in their lives for which they had failed to distinguish, admit or seek help.

As I pointed this out to them they both understood, and, with the help of God, they began to repent, renounce, and pray for a complete release of all generational curses. The first step is always to recognize that there is a problem. After the problem is recognized, then repentance must come and to repent means to turn from, not just say I'm sorry. The turning from can be a problem, too, as we found in this particular situation. The turning from one problem resulted in turning into an entirely different problem. That is the very reason we need to recognize it as a generational curse, or iniquity, and break from that once and for all.

CURSES ACQUIRED FROM CULTURE

Some years ago we were ministering in one of the islands in the Caribbean where we found curses abounding due to the culture. During this time we went to the islands about four times a year and ministering through prayer groups, churches, Women's Aglow, and Full Gospel Businessmen's Fellowship. As we researched the history of the island, we found that when Columbus came over to America in the 1400s that he probably landed on one of these islands. He reported that it was an uninhabited island with great green sea turtles everywhere. (Even today there are still big turtles there.)

Since the island had no native peoples, when pirating was at it greatest peak, this island was a haven for pirates, for the only access to the island was on the south side and they could be protected. Ships coming from the east would hit the coral barriers and wreck. The north side was too shallow for ships to come in, and the harbor that is now on the west end of the island had not been dredged at that time. The results were that the pirates took over the island for their hideout, and the iniquity handed down for the last four or five hundred years is still in effect over the older residents.

One of the most prevalent curses is barrenness among women of child-bearing age. In their culture having children is most important in all families. They feel it is necessary to have children to make their lives complete. At the end of meetings or church services, it was my custom to ask any of the ladies who wished to have children to come forward for prayer. It seemed there were always several. My husband and I would lay hands on them, break the iniquity, and pray that each of them would be productive. God honored our prayers and the success rate was phenomenal.

On one of our trips down to the islands we were having dinner with a couple from England who lived there. They had invited an unsaved couple to join us for dinner so we would have the chance to witness to them and see what God would do. The dinner was going well, we had witnessed to them, and they were receiving all the things we had said when there was a loud knock on the door. Immediately, the door burst open and in came a large lady who was obviously pregnant. I recognized her as one we had prayed for six months previous when we had made our trip to the island.

"Brother Clouse," she practically shouted as she rushed in and gave my surprised husband a big hug, "You're the one who made me pregnant." I laughed uproariously and then sputtered and tried to explain to our guests just what she meant. The lady with the news looked bewildered and would not be silenced for she was so excited about her glorious announcement.

Another encounter with barrenness occurred with a very close friend of mine from Sweden who lived on the island. She had met an American gentleman and they fell in love and married. He had been married before and had grown children from a previous marriage. She had never had children and desperately wanted a child. She shared this with me at prayer time after a Women's Aglow meeting where I was speaking. I broke all curses off her and prayed healing for all her internal organs. She wept much, for she felt she was too old to bear for she was almost past the child-bearing age.

After the prayer she had to go to the ladies' room and began to pass a brown substance. She said it was just as if a doctor had gone in and scraped the womb. She was excited and filled with hope. Within that month she became pregnant—to God be the glory! We returned to the island just nine months later and were there when their beautiful baby girl was born. God is able to do exceeding abundantly above all that we ask or think.

Things in my life changed during this time and I did not get to return to this island. Even though we did not get to return and see it with our own eyes we have had reports through mutual friends as this little girl has grown to adulthood. God is so good and His intention is to bless us in all situations. The sad part of the story was that the father died with a heart attack, but he did get to see his beautiful little daughter in her first three years of life.

CURSES DUE TO VOODOO AND WITCHCRAFT

The more we ministered in the Caribbean, the more we recognized the results of iniquities that had been handed down for generations. Some of our African-born brothers came to the island and some of the curses of voodoo came along as well. The voodoo practiced in the islands is called *obia*, and this has been known to include human sacrifice, as well as animal sacrifice. The internal organs of chickens, as well as small animals, are used in their rituals for spell casting and many other practices.

With the history of voodoo and pirates, we recognized the "curse of the sea" as it fell on some people. One teenager from the island, a young lady of perhaps nineteen, had skin that was cracked and looked more like fish scales than skin. The locals said this was from the curse of the sea. Bondage seemed to be rampant, but the good part was that as soon as people got revelation, they accepted correction and submitted their lives to God.

One of the interesting things manifested was when we made a trip to the eastern end of the island. This area was quite depressed and entirely unlike the western end, where the harbor is located. The people in this area did not have any kind of health care at that time, and many needs were evident. Some of the Christian residents in the western town would make a trip each week to the eastern end of the island to take groceries and such to the needy families. My husband and I made the trip many times. We prayed for people as we dispensed the groceries.

On one such trip we saw a cabin tucked back away from the road. We had to walk quite a way to the house, each of us carrying a bag of groceries. As we climbed over the coral rocks to the front door, it looked as if no one were home. When people on the island were home, they typically left their front doors open. However, our guide (I'll call her Ginny) insisted that the lady was home. She was a single mother and had five children, and one of them was having major problems. Ginny said he was about six years old, and she felt we should make an all-out effort to pray for him.

We knocked on the door and a lively female voice responded immediately, "I'll be there in just a moment."

The door swung open quickly, displaying a barren room holding only a worn sofa. Ginny smiled broadly and said, "The evangelists from the states are here. We have some groceries for you and they wish to pray for your son."

At this point I saw the little boy scramble across the room toward the door with a wild look in his eyes. Not only were his eyes wild looking, but the rest of him looked wild as well. He was on all fours—hands and feet—for all the world acting like a wild animal. The mother immediately slammed the front door so he would not escape out of the house. The only thing I could think was, "That poor, precious child!" My husband later said all he could think was, "That's not a child. It may appear to be a child according to my eyes, but in reality it's more of a monkey or some other small animal than it is a child."

Ginny was determined to catch the boy so we could pray for him, so she dived at the boy's legs as he came close to the door, but he evaded her and circled the room at full gallop. "Help me catch him," she called to my husband, and he immediately joined the chase. At this point my eyes saw things that I still have doubts about and cannot fully explain. As they chased this little boy around and around the room, he continued to evade them. As they would get him cornered and seemed sure to snare him, he would literally go up and across the wall, and then back down to the floor. The mother was spending her time wailing and trying to get him to stop so we could pray for him.

When it finally seemed as if they would never catch him, Ginny got him by one foot. My husband immediately latched onto the other, and then I ploughed right in and prayed for him. I rebuked every demon I could think of, broke all generational curses, and asked for the peace of Jesus to come on him. Within a matter of minutes he settled right down and smiled at me. His mother said he had never been able to talk and was always wild, but was not always as wild as he had been that day. Within a ten-minute time span he was sitting on the sofa with me as I told him a story about Jesus. He even repeated after me "Jesus" as I encouraged him. We never did know for sure what the demonic stronghold in his life was, but we do know that Jesus touched him that day.

As we completed our visit, the boy's mother walked to the door with us as we started our trudge back to the main road where we had left the car. As we looked back, she and her little boy were standing together in the doorway waving. The door could now be left open for he was no longer the wild, little, animal-like boy who was there when we arrived. Less than an hour had passed and yet their lives had been changed.

As we neared the car we saw a lady standing there holding a small child. The child was lying limply in her arms. It was a little girl and she was perhaps two years old. On her head was a white cloth, tied at the four corners, and you could see it was damp.

"Are you praying for sick people, today?" she asked.

"We most assuredly are," I quickly answered. "What's wrong with your baby?" I asked her.

"She has a fever."

"What is that cloth on her head?" I asked out of curiosity.

"It's just a handkerchief," her mother answered. "I put salve on it and put it on her head to help with the fever." (We don't know for sure, but we assume the salve was Vaseline or Vicks).

As I gently laid my hand on the little girl's forehead I could feel the heat and thought to myself that her temperature must be at least 102 or higher. I rebuked the fever in the name of Jesus, broke generational curses, and prayed for complete healing from the top of her head to the bottom of her feet.

Immediately the mother said, "Amen!," set the little girl down, and said, "Go on. Run and play." The little girl scampered off toward where her brothers and sisters were. Being an American, I wanted to say, "Wait a minute, and let's see if the fever is gone," but somehow I knew that was not the right thing to do. The mother had set the child down in faith, never doubting that she was healed. We, in America, need to learn that lesson.

LET DOWN YOUR NETS

The Lord showed me a scripture the other day that revealed His heart to me. In Luke 5:4 He was speaking to the multitudes. Picking up in verse 4 the Bible says: "When He had stopped speaking, He said to Simon, 'Launch out into the deep and let *down your nets* for a catch.' But Simon answered and said to Him, 'Master, we have toiled all night and caught nothing; nevertheless at Your word I will let *down the net*'" (emphasis mine). You will note that Jesus said to let *down your nets*, plural, and Peter said he would let *down the net,* singular.

Let's continue in verse 6 and 7.

> "And when they had done this, they caught a great number of fish, and their net (again singular) was breaking. So they signaled to their partners in the other boat to come and help them. And they came and filled both the boats, so that they began to sink."

Jesus tried to tell them they needed more than one net. Still, even though they only partially obeyed the Lord, He did abundantly more than they could imagine. Isn't that just like God? He always does more than we think He will. Not only that, He isn't vindictive and doesn't rebuke us when we have a lack in complete faith.

The clincher on this is in verse 8:

> When Simon Peter saw it, he fell down at Jesus' knees, saying, "Depart from me, for I am a sinful man, O Lord!"

He had a revelation and was astonished at the catch of fish they had taken. Jesus answered him and said, "Do not be afraid," and that is what He is still saying to us today. Do not be afraid, just get the revelation, break generational curses and get rid of iniquities, and walk in victory for the rest of your life.

I am reminded of Proverbs 5:21–23:

> "For the ways of man are before the eyes of the Lord, and He ponders all his paths. His own iniquities entrap the wicked man, and he is caught in the cords of his sin. He shall die for lack of instruction, and in the greatness of his folly he shall go astray."

What a blessing it is to see the islanders receive from the Lord as their iniquities are revealed to them.

CHAPTER 6

Repent of the Sin

— iniquity = continually repeated sin! —

Many people tell God they are sorry. They even go to the altar and cry and ask Him to forgive them, which He does. But afterward, they do not turn from the sin they committed. The result is iniquity.

A sin that is repeatedly committed becomes an iniquity that can be passed down through the bloodline. When a person continually transgresses the law, iniquity is created in him and that iniquity is passed to his children. The offspring will have a weakness (or bend) toward the same kind of sin—especially under certain circumstances. Each generation adds to the overall iniquity, further weakening the resistance of the next generation to sin. As the resistance is weakened, the sin becomes worse and worse. The acts of sin are spontaneous, automatic, habitual. History tells us that man's depravity continues to get worse, unless God comes in and changes that life. It takes the blood of Jesus to cleanse us or we will continue our downward slide.

Repentance (turning from the sin) must come if we are to be set free and never face the iniquity again. Repenting means to ask forgiveness, as well as to stop sinning, turn 180 degrees, and go in the opposite direction. God does not consider it enough to just ask forgiveness for the sin. He also requires that we turn from it.

God has shown us in the Old Testament, in many passages, the importance of repenting of iniquities. We read in 2 Chronicles 7:14: "If My people who are called by My name will humble themselves, and pray and seek My face, and turn from their wicked ways, then I will hear from heaven, and will forgive their sin and heal their land." If we do our part, then He will forgive the sin, which in turn gets rid of the iniquity. What a deal He has given us! If we know His promise, why would we ever fail to fulfill the requirements?

An example of someone repenting of iniquities of the entire nation is in the Book of Daniel. Daniel was a young man who had been taken captive, made into a eunuch, which meant he would never marry or father a family. He had not sinned. He had not rebelled. Yet, in his prayer to God he said "we" have sinned. He did not say "the kings, princes and fathers have sinned." He said "we" have sinned.

> In the first year of Darius' reign, I, Daniel, understood by the books the number of the years specified by the word of the Lord through Jeremiah the prophet, that He would accomplish seventy years in the desolations of Jerusalem. Then I set my face toward the Lord God to make request by prayer and supplications, with fasting, sackcloth, and ashes.
>
> And I prayed to the Lord my God, and made

confession, and said, "O Lord, great and awesome God, who keeps His covenant and mercy with those who love Him, and with those who keep His commandments, *we* have sinned and committed iniquity, *we* have done wickedly and rebelled, even by departing from Your precepts and Your judgments. Neither have *we* heeded Your servants the prophets, who spoke in Your name to our kings and our princes, to our fathers and all the people of the land.

"O Lord, righteousness belongs to You, but to us shame of face, as it is this day — to the men of Judah, to the inhabitants of Jerusalem and all Israel, those near and those far off in all the countries to which You have driven them, because of the unfaithfulness which they have committed against you. O Lord, to us belongs shame of face, to our kings, our princes, and our fathers, because we have sinned against You.

"To the Lord our God belong mercy and forgiveness, though *we* have rebelled against Him. *We* have not obeyed the voice of the Lord our God, to walk in His laws, which He set before us by His servants the prophets. Yes, all Israel has transgressed Your law, and has departed so as not to obey Your voice; therefore the curse and the oath written in the Law of Moses the servant of God have been poured out on us, because *we* have sinned against Him."

—DANIEL 9:2–11, ITALICS ADDED

Daniel was fasting and praying to break the iniquity of the people for they were in bondage. He had read the prophecy of Jeremiah and knew by the reading of it that it was time for the people to come out of bondage. Then he concluded: "O Lord, hear! O Lord, forgive! O Lord, listen and act! Do not delay for Your own sake, my God, for Your city and Your people are called by Your name" (v. 19).

Because of this prayer the angel Gabriel answered and said: "O Daniel, I have now come forth to give you skill to understand. At the beginning of your supplications the command went out and I have come to tell you, for you are greatly beloved; therefore consider the matter, and understand the vision" (v. 22).

Then Gabriel told him God's answer to his request: "Seventy weeks are determined for your people and for your holy city, to finish the transgression, to make an end of sins, to make reconciliation for iniquity." And, yes, Israel was brought out of bondage. The Lord made sure this account was placed in the Bible, so we would know what to do when we are in bondage. He gave us a pattern to follow so we would know how to pray and get loosed from bondage.

NEHEMIAH'S REPENTANCE

It's important to understand that God does not *blame* us for the sins of our fathers; however, we do suffer the consequences of their sin. Nehemiah confessed both his own sins and the sins of his father's house when he fasted and prayed before God.

> I pray, Lord God of heaven, O great and awe-some God, You who keep Your covenant and mercy with those who love You and observe Your com-mandments, please let Your ear be attentive and Your eyes open, that You may hear the prayer of Your servant which I pray before You now, day and night, for the children of Israel Your servants, and

confess the sins of the children of Israel which we
have sinned against You. Both my father's house
and I have sinned.

—NEHEMIAH 1:5–6

Nehemiah pleaded, "Oh, God, have mercy on *us.*"
Nehemiah could have said, "I didn't do anything wrong!
I don't have to confess the things they did." But he recognized the mystery of iniquity at work in the bloodline.
Nehemiah realized that he had an inclination towards the
iniquity of which his fathers and the nation of Israel were
guilty.

Nehemiah confessed the iniquity and then reminded
God of His promise:

> We have acted very corruptly against You, and
> have not kept the commandments, the statutes, nor
> the ordinances which You commanded Your servant
> Moses. Remember, I pray, the word that You com-
> manded Your servant Moses, saying, "If you are
> unfaithful, I will scatter you among the nations; but
> if you return to Me, and keep My commandments
> and do them, though some of you were cast out to
> the farthest part of the heavens, yet I will gather
> them from there, and bring them to the place which
> I have chosen as a dwelling for My name."
>
> —vv. 7–9

Nehemiah fasted, prayed, and repented, saying *we*
have sinned. The Lord heeded that prayer and Nehemiah
was sent back to Judah. The repenting is a necessary part
and must come before freedom can be realized. Also
notice that he reminded God of His word that He would
bring them back to their own land. (Israel was more prosperous than ever before in history).

After Nehemiah's prayer, the king of Persia let him go back and rebuild the walls and the gates and made provision for building supplies and workers. When we can use the devil's money to build the walls and gates of our city—that is true prosperity. They finished building in fifty-two days. The most prosperous time in Israel's history was the next four hundred years. Why? Because if you *cover* the sins of your family you will not prosper, but if you *confess* your sins and the sins of your family, both you and your family will prosper. It only takes one person to repent to change the course of history for a whole nation.

MODERN-DAY REPENTANCE

An example of modern-day repenting and asking forgiveness was made by Pope John Paul II in March of 2000. On the second Sunday in March, he asked God's forgiveness for sins committed or condoned by Roman Catholics during the past two thousand years, including sexism, racism, hatred of Jews and violence in defense of the Catholic faith. He asked the church to enter the third millennium with a pure conscience as he interceded on their behalf for victims including heretics, Protestants, Jews and other non-Christians, immigrants, ethnic minorities, women, abused children as well as the unborn.

Several times during his day of Pardon Mass in St. Peter's Basilica he said, "We forgive and ask forgiveness." This initiative by the Pope to bring about reconciliation was welcomed by most people worldwide. "We ask forgiveness for the divisions among Christians, for the use of violence that some Christians have committed in the service of the truth and for the attitudes of mistrust and hostility sometimes assumed toward followers of other religions." (Source: *Orlando Sentinel*)

This repeting and asking forgiveness for sins committed over the past two thousand years shows us just how far iniquities can go. In fact, they can go even further unless we repent and break the cycle. Generational sins can be thought of as cycles, for they are just like a wheel, continually going in a circle, around and around, year after year, until they are broken through the power of God.

ASKING FORGIVENESS VS. REPENTANCE

I will relate to you a story of a lady friend of mine, and her battle with sin. She was saved, Spirit-filled and trying to live for the Lord. Her husband had divorced her, and she raised their two children to the best of her ability. Her story shows us how the devil tries to make us think that repentance isn't necessary.

After some years, her children were grown and on their own so she decided to attend a Christian seminar in a nearby city. It was a great seminar, and she was enjoying herself.

At the end of the afternoon session, she was in a nearby restaurant, when in walked a fine-looking gentleman, looking for a table. All the tables were occupied, so he asked if he might join her as he was alone. She agreed, in fact, welcomed the company, for she was feeling somewhat lonely. As they chatted, they found they had a lot in common. They were both attending the same seminar, and both lived in the same city nearby. She had come alone, and he also had come alone. He was married, but his wife did not like religious conferences so she had stayed home. In fact, he confided, he and his wife had very little in common.

They got their food orders and continued to enjoy each other's company. As they paid their bills he asked where she was staying. She named the hotel nearby and he said he was staying at the same hotel. They walked back together, then each went to their respective rooms to get a little rest and refreshing before the next scheduled session.

As she came out of her room and went to the elevator to ride to the ground floor, the door opened and there he was, on his way to the meeting. They greeted each other warmly and went on to the meeting. The two of them seemed to hit it off and discussed the meeting and each person that was ministering. They were quickly becoming warm friends.

After the meeting that night they went out for a snack, and the more they talked the more they seemed to have in common. (Temptation is strongest when we are vulnerable, need company, and the right temptation comes along). As they went back to the hotel that night, he walked her to her room and kissed her goodnight. It seemed to be the most natural thing in the world, but she did feel a twinge of guilt.

The next morning they met for breakfast, as each of them were anxious to see the other. After breakfast they went back to the hotel, for there was no morning meeting. Again he walked her to her room door, and she invited him in so they could share some time together. As they were in the intimacy of the hotel room, the inevitable happened. They had sex.

Afterward he knelt by the bed to pray and ask God to forgive him. She also cried and asked God to forgive her and help her to never commit that sin again. He looked at her rather strangely and said: "I asked God to forgive me and He did. That's all there is to it."

They went downstairs and went to lunch and then on to the meeting. She had a hard time in the meeting, for she was still remembering the sin, but he seemed to be his regular old self. After the afternoon meeting he wanted to go back to her room, but she refused to allow him in. She went in alone and cried and repented again.

After the night meeting that night they again went out for a meal together, and upon returning to the hotel, he talked her into again going to her room. Again they fell into sin, and again he knelt by the bed and asked God to forgive him. His theology was not like hers at all.

"If you ask God to forgive you, then He is faithful and just to forgive you," he stated quite emphatically. "If I sin again, I'll just ask forgiveness again."

She answered him, "I think you are right in the fact that He will forgive you if you sin, but if you do not repent, but just keep on sinning, and doing the same thing over and over, then that is a different matter entirely."

This good friend of mine came back after that conference and asked for counseling. She even arranged for this man to come with her. That was some session we had.

"Do you have plans to leave your wife, or does she plan to leave you?" I asked him.

"Of course not," he answered. "We don't get along, but we have children and property that I do not want to break up."

"Then what are your intentions toward my friend?"

"I don't see anything wrong with continuing to see her," he answered. "I am a good Christian, go to church every Sunday. I ask God to forgive me when I sin. What more should I do?"

"When you are in sin, you can be deceived," I told him. "God wants you to ask forgiveness for your sin, but He also wants you to *repent* and turn from that way and sin no more. Jesus always said to the people He ministered to: 'Be made whole! Go and sin no more.' That's what repent means."

I regret to say that I could not convince him to stop his sinning. I did convince my friend, however, and she is now happily married to a fine man and they continue to serve the Lord.

SOUL TIES

I feel that at this point I should discuss *soul ties* and how to break them. Soul ties are formed when we are emotionally involved with a person. Even after we have severed the relationship and no longer associate with that person, we can still be so bound to them that we think of them longingly and our soul yearns for them. Of course, as we have said before, our soul is our mind, our will, and our emotions. All three of these can be tied up with a person we no longer associate with, for a variety of reasons.

Most especially this is true if we have been sexually involved with the person—whether in the context of a legal marriage or an immoral sexual escapade. A soul tie is so strong that it must be broken to set the person free.

David asked the Lord to heal his soul. "I said, 'Lord, be merciful to me; Heal my soul, for I have sinned against You'" (Ps. 41:4). Soul ties are like an umbilical cord. They tie your mind to another person. Even though my friend stopped sinning, simply having any contact with this man would bring back the longing for his companionship. An emotional tie had formed since they enjoyed each other. (Emotional ties cause a person to long for what used to be.) Realizing that she was not free in her soul, she took the following steps to totally break all bondages and soul ties.

Use these steps to set yourself free.

1. Repentance towards God for the sin.
2. Confess as sin all promiscuous behavior (premarital sex, adultery, etc.)
3. Loose yourself from all soulish ties to past relationships. Uproot all the tentacles of sexual

bondage of emotional longings, dependencies and enslaving of thoughts.

4. Bind, renounce, and resist all evil spirits that have been transferred to you through evil associations.
5. Command all evil spirits associated with soul ties to leave you in Jesus' name.
6. Put you hand on your heart and ask the Lord to heal the wounds in your soul. Ask that ever fragmented piece of your heart be restored by the healing power in the name of Jesus.

I will give you a sample prayer to pray to break soul ties with anyone with whom you have been involved.

Father, in the name of Jesus, I submit my soul, my desires, and my emotions to your Spirit. I confess, as sin, all premarital sexual relationships and all sexual relationships outside of marriage. I confess all my ungodly spirit, soul, and body ties as sin. I thank You for forgiving me and cleansing me right now! Thank You for giving me the keys of Your kingdom, the keys of spiritual authority. What I bind is bound and what I loose is loosed. In Jesus' name, I ask You to loose me from all soulish ties to past sexual partners and ungodly relationships. Please uproot all the tentacles of sexual bondage, of emotional longings and dependencies, and of enslaving thoughts. I bind, renounce, and resist any evil spirits that have reinforced those soul ties or may have been transferred to me through evil associations.

Please cleanse my soul and help me to forget all illicit unions so that I am free to give my soul totally to You and my mate. Father, I receive Your forgiveness for all past sex sins. I believe I am totally forgiven. Thank You for remembering my sins no more and for cleansing me. I commit myself totally to You. By Your grace, please keep me holy in spirit, soul, and body. I praise You. In Jesus' name, amen.

CONCLUSION

True repentance is totally turning away from sin.

Judas Iscariot wept bitter tears after he had betrayed Jesus. It is very plain in the Word that he did not repent, but instead committed suicide. Peter denied Jesus, cut off a man's ear, slept when he should have been praying, left his calling as a disciple and returned to fishing.

Peter and Judas were both close to Jesus. Both sinned. One did not turn away from his sin and died. The other turned away from his sin by confessing his love for Jesus and went on to live a victorious live. Peter learned not only to repent of his sin, he also learned to renounce any involvement with sin.

....

CHAPTER 7

Renounce Involvement

My husband's son was the last of his children to receive salvation. He had always been a little bit wild as he was growing up. As we prayed for him for salvation and then later for the baptism in the Holy Spirit, we discovered some openings that Satan used to harass him.

He had gone to a school-related party when he was twelve or thirteen years old and they were playing games. One of the games they were playing involved one of his classmates who was dressed as a fortune-teller. She had no training or experience in that area and they felt it was a harmless game. When she read his palm, she said, "You have an extremely short lifeline. You will not live to be thirty years of age." Even though he knew it was just a game, it had a profound effect upon him. (In reality, it was a curse placed upon him). From that day forward he was erratic and wild. He was sure, even though he never told anyone, that his life would be short, so what difference did it make anyway?

As he told us about this, he laughed, for he knew the girl who pronounced the curse very well, and even so, she was only playing the game. At the time we did not realize the critical importance of renouncing involvement, but decided we would do it to be on the safe side. He repented of the sin of fortune-telling, and then we led him in a prayer of release from involvement in the so-called game.

We know now that we did the right thing at that time. His life, as well as his entire family, has been blessed and not cursed. He has lived to see his children, as well as his grandchildren, and he still has many years still ahead. Praise God!

WHEN DO YOU RENOUNCE?

There is a subtle difference between repenting and renouncing. Repenting means to stop sinning and go in the other direction. We need to repent of whatever initially exposed us to the curse, whether it was our own sin or the sin of our ancestors. Renouncing means you cast off any involvement in activities that invited Satan's activity in your life. These activities include involvement in the occult, reading your horoscope, playing the Ouija board, going to a medium or having your fortune read. Renouncing should be done verbally—out loud. If you have been involved in any of these, renounce all involvement, and cleanse your house by removing all objects from the occult.

I am frequently asked, "Why is it necessary for me to not only repent, but also to say with my mouth, 'I renounce any involvement in the breaking of God's commandments'"? My answer always goes back to the Word. Numbers 14:18 says, "The Lord is longsuffering and abundant in mercy, forgiving iniquity and transgression; but he by no means clears the guilty, visiting the iniquity of the fathers on the children to the third and fourth generation."

This verse says that God does not clear the guilty, so how can we ever get set free? The solution came through Jesus' death on the cross. In Isaiah 53:5 we are told: "He was wounded for our transgressions, He was bruised for our iniquities." Jesus took our iniquity upon Himself, in order to break the hold the devil has on us.

When you renounce you are actually saying to Satan, "I break your hold on me. I can be free of this iniquity by the blood of Jesus. Your legal hold on me is broken." If at any time we have succumbed to Satan's attack in generational iniquities we should renounce it. When there is an iniquity in our past, Satan feels he has a legal right to be involved in our lives, and he continues to harass us in this particular area. It is necessary for us to renounce any involvement in any area in which Satan has been active. For example, if you have a generational bend toward lying, and Satan has tempted you in that area, and you have succumbed, you need to renounce lying.

The need to renounce is obvious when we read Jesus' teaching about the strong man: "If I cast out demons by the Spirit of God, surely the kingdom of God has come upon you. Or how can one enter a strong man's house and plunder his goods, unless he first binds the strong man? And then he will plunder his house" (Matt. 12:28–29). If we hope to overcome Satan, then we must bind him, cast him out, and walk on in freedom.

ENTHRONING JESUS

If and when we cooperate with the devil, we "give place" to him. We actually enthrone him in our lives.

"Do you not know that to whom you present yourselves slaves to obey, you are that one's slaves whom you obey, whether of sin leading to death, or of obedience leading to righteousness" (Rom. 6:16).

Every time a person lies, cheats, or gives in to lustful thoughts, the dominion of Satan in and/or through that life has been strengthened. In the same way, I can enthrone Jesus by obeying His Word and His will. I make decisions continually concerning whom I will enthrone in my life. It is the power of Christ's life in me that enables me to choose correctly and carry out the obedience of God in my life. When we exercise our power of choice it establishes us in our authority.

The body of Christ has too long been paralyzed by not understanding the power we exercise daily in our choices. Though the world has enthroned the right of man to choose, the church has abdicated her true authority by not choosing to obey the Word. The power that determines the outcome of the battle in every case is man's power of choice, not the devil's power or might.

SATAN'S POWER IS ILLEGITIMATE

Through repentance and renouncing, we loose Satan's power over us and take back what the enemy has stolen from us. In reality, Satan has no legitimate power of his own. Jesus disarmed him of all his power and authority. "Having wiped out the handwriting of requirements that was against us, which was contrary to us. And He has taken it out of the way, having nailed it to the cross. Having disarmed principalities and powers, He made a public spectacle of them, triumphing over them in it" (Col. 2:14–15).

Not only did Christ disarm Satan, spoiling principalities and powers in open triumph, He also purposed to destroy him. "Inasmuch then as the children have partaken of flesh and blood, He Himself likewise shared in the same, that through death He might destroy him who had the power of death, that is, the devil" (Heb. 2:14).

Not only did He come to destroy the devil, He came to destroy the works of the devil. "For this purpose the Son of God was manifested, that He might destroy the works of the devil" (1 John 3:8). Satan had the power of death, but Revelation says Christ took the keys of hell and death. It is clear that Jesus has authority over Satan, and the good news is that Jesus transferred that authority to mankind so that they could overcome evil. Jesus told His disciples: "Behold, I give you the authority to trample on serpents and scorpions, and over all the power of the enemy, and nothing shall by any means hurt you" (Luke 10:19). We can, by this, see that the devil has no legitimate power of his own.

Then where does he get his power? He usurps his power from man's wrong choices. When we do not choose to believe the truth and fight the fight of faith, we relinquish our power to the devil. It would do us all a lot of good to take this statement and post it on our refrigerator or in a prominent place where we could read it daily.

The only power Satan has is what he siphons out of our tank of authority. The truth is that Christ has given all authority over the power of the devil to us. Therefore, the devil must wait for us to default from our position of victory in order to exercise any oppressive, destructive, power against us.

The bottom line is this: to break generational curses, we have to make a choice. Our will is the thing involved. God won't cross your will and Satan can't. You have to choose Jesus! To get set free you must want to be set free.

We need to realize that truth is the revelation of God's Word. We need to acknowledge truth in our inner self. As a Christian, we should renounce deception and embrace the truth. Don't let the enemy accuse you with thoughts such as: "This isn't going to work" or "I wish I could believe this but I can't" or any other lies in opposition to what you are proclaiming. Even if you have difficulty doing so, you need to pray a prayer of release and get set completely free of all curses, regardless of the origin.

DEMONIC GATEWAYS OF OPPORTUNITY

Curses are enforced by demons or demonic spirits. They put the curse into effect, so to speak. However, demons cannot enter at will. They must have a legal right, or a gateway of opportunity. No one can put a curse on us unless there is an opening in our lives. Jesus said in Matthew 12 that the "Spirit of God" casts out the demons. When God's conditions have been met, a demon has no right to stay. Let's look at this a little deeper.

Watch what you buy in foreign countries. One of my friends purchased a beautiful stone called a "good luck rock" while on a trip to Greece. It was very pretty and looked nice in her house. The rock was supposed to bring wealth. Instead it brought poverty. The door was opened for Satan to come in and steal, kill and destroy because the rock she brought into her home was an occult object that represented a false god.

She is an accountant, but she did not have a good job. For six months we had prayed many times for her to get a better job. After hearing me teach on blessings and curses, she brought the rock for me to examine. After an examination we decided to destroy the rock. Within two weeks she was employed as an accountant, which doubled her salary.

When she repented of idolatry and renounced it, she broke the entrance into her life for demonic influences to enter. Destroying the rock removed the legal entrance that had been given to Satan by bringing an idol into the home.

HONORING PARENTS

At many conferences I teach a workshop on honoring your parents. In Ephesians 6:1–3, we are told to obey our parents if we want to live a long and peaceful life. This is a commandment with a promise of God's blessing. After one workshop, a young lady come to me and said, "I cannot honor my parents because my mother is a witch. I have been saved about six months, and I don't want to be around her."

As we talked, I learned that this young lady had numerous physical problems, financial difficulties and her husband had been diagnosed with cancer. I explained to her that until we forgive others who may have hurt us, that God cannot forgive us. That bitterness and unforgiveness leaves the door open for Satan to march in and out of our lives as he wills. She followed me in a prayer to forgive her mother and we agreed for salvation for her and her household. She asked the Lord to forgive her and her mother for their involvement in witchcraft. I had her renounce any involvement in the occult. By renouncing, a person literally breaks Satan's legal authority that she has given him in her life.

One year later she returned to the *Charisma* Women's Conference and attended my workshop again. She had a big smile on her face and a great testimony. Her husband had been healed, her mother was saved and their finances had greatly improved. The curse was reversed by following God's requirements.

THE FOUR "R" STEPS

Let's review the first three steps in breaking a generational curse.

1. **Recognize.** Unless we recognize that we have a problem we will never go any further to get set free, so the first step is to recognize the curse.

2. **Repent.** We must repent of whatever initially exposed us to the problem, whether it was our own sin or the sin of our ancestors. Remember that repent means to stop sinning and go in the opposite direction.

3. **Renounce.** We must say, "It no longer belongs to me. I do not accept it. Through the blood of Jesus I have been liberated from the curse of the law. I am free through the name and blood of Jesus Christ."

Now we are ready for step 4:

4. **Release.** We must take a very definite active stand against the power of Satan and resist him with a prayer of release.

The next chapter gives you powerful prayer guidelines for this key step.

CHAPTER 8

··

Pray a Prayer
of Release

The Bible says in Proverbs 18:21: "Death and life are in the power of the tongue," and praying a prayer of release is a necessity in getting released from generational curses. To have life and have it more abundantly there must be a prayer of release *spoken*.

To release means "to liberate, to be relieved from care, pain, trouble; discharge from an obligation, as from a debt." God wants to totally liberate you from the pain of past hurts and present circumstances. His plan for you is to set you free from guilt and shame.

I am giving you several samples of prayers that needs to be prayed. You don't have to use the same exact words, but words similar to these should be used to completely free you from generational cycles, so that you will never be bothered again.

In order to pray a prayer of release, you need to specifically identify the cause of the curses in your life so that you can speak your release from them. To help you, I will again list the common causes of curses. The ones that apply to you, perhaps all of them, need to be prayed over and released by you. As you recognize the problem, repent of the sin, renounce (cast off) and as you pray the prayer of release you are going to feel the bondage and chains broken off your life.

1. Idolatry, false gods, the occult. Deuteronomy 27:15 speaks of making false gods: "Cursed is the one who makes a carved or molded image, an abomination to the Lord, the work of the hands of the craftsman, and sets it up in secret." Deuteronomy 18:9–12 warns against occult practices: "When you come into the land which the Lord your God is giving you, you shall not learn to follow the abominations of those nations. There shall not be found among you anyone who makes his son or his daughter pass through the fire, or one who practices witchcraft (KJV says "useth divination,") or a soothsayer (KJV says "an observer of times,") or one who interprets omens, or a sorcerer, or one who conjures spells, or a medium, or a spiritist, or one who calls up the dead. For all who do these things are an abomination to the Lord, and because of these abominations the Lord your God drives them out from before you." In modern times, these practices would include ESP, fortune-telling and consulting a medium or horoscope.

2. Dishonoring parents.

3. Illicit or unnatural sex. These practices include adultery (sex or lusting after another person to whom you are not married), fornication (sex before marriage), bestiality (sex with an animal; see Deuteronomy 27:21).

4. Injustice to the weak or helpless. The supreme example of injustice in our society today is procuring a deliberate abortion.

5. Trusting in the arm of flesh. This is when you think

you are sufficient within yourself and don't need God.

6. Stealing or perjury.

7. Being stingy with God financially. Malachi 3:10 says, "Bring all the tithes into the storehouse."

8. Negative words spoken by persons with relational authority, such as: parents, husbands, teachers or pastors.

9. Self-imposed curses. These are curses that people pronounce upon themselves. ("I will never amount to anything," "I am just like my father or mother," and so on.)

10. Words pronounced by persons representing Satan, such as: witch doctors, etc.

11. Soulish prayers, utterances spoken in wrong attitudes, and gossip.

12. Unscriptural covenants. Being united by covenant with people who are aligned with forces that are evil and alien to God, for example, Freemasonry, Christian Science, etc.

Many more that could be listed, but these are the ones most commonly brought up.

Once we have identified the cause or source of the curse we (or, in many cases, our ancestors or others associated with us) were exposed to, we must take a definite stand against Satan and resist him with a prayer of release.

The prayer of release could be something like this.

> *Dear Jesus:*
>
> *I believe that You are the Son of God and the only way to God; that on the cross You died for my sins; and that You rose again from the dead; that on the cross also You were made a curse, that I might be redeemed from the curse and receive Your blessing.*
>
> *I trust you now for mercy and forgiveness and I commit myself from now on by Your grace to follow and obey You.*

Heavenly Father,

I ask You to guard my heart and mind and reveal to me any and all involvement I have had, either knowingly or unknowingly, with cultic or occult practices, false religions or false teachers. I set aside all previous or preconceived ideas and ask You to speak to me now so that I may be set free from all bondages.

[Pause for a minute and give the Lord a chance to speak to you. Now continue with the following prayer.]

I ask for Your mercy and forgiveness. I ask You to forgive and blot out any sins committed by me or by my ancestors that exposed me to a curse

[At this point, name any specific sins of which you are aware].

If people have harmed me or wronged me, I forgive them, as I would have God to forgive me.

[Name these people. It could been a school teacher, a parent, a mate, or some other person.]

I renounce all contact with Satan, occult practices, and unscriptural secret societies. If I have any contact objects that link me to these things, I promise to destroy them.

[Name the specific practices and/or secret societies with which you were involved.]

Satan, in the name of Jesus I recognize your plan to destroy me, and I repent of any sin that caused me to bring shame to the name of Jesus. In the name of Jesus you have no right to my life and no power over me. I belong to God and will serve Him and Him only. By the authority of my Lord Jesus Christ, I renounce and break the power of every evil curse that has come upon me. I command every demon associated with the curse to leave me now: ancestral curse spirits, personal transgression, witchcraft curse spirits, word curses, spirit of heaviness, spirit of whoredom, spirit of infirmity, dumb and deaf spirit (under this comes insanity, schizophrenia, seizures, suicide), spirit of fear, spirit of pride, spirit of bondage, spirit of anti-Christ, spirit of perversion, familiar spirits, spirit of lying, spirit of jealousy, religious spirits, control and manipulation, spirit of rage, spirit of competition, judgmental and critical spirits . . . I loose myself from all bondage. Now, I thank You, Lord, that I am free from the curses. In Jesus' name, amen.

You can be confident that your prayer has made an impact in the spiritual realm because Jesus said, "Assuredly, I say to you, whatever you bind on earth will be bound in heaven, and whatever you loose on earth will be loosed in heaven" (Matt 18:18).

SEVEN STEPS TO FREEDOM

God wants to completely set you free from the bondage of the past. As you look over these seven steps to freedom, you will see that they were all used in the prayer of release. Saying the prayer aloud has a powerful impact in the spiritual realm. Now to keep yourself free from attack, stay in obedience to these seven principles.

1. Put your faith in God's Word. Your faith must be based on God's Word (Eph. 1:7) and Jesus' blood (Col. 1:13–14).
2. Confess your faith in Christ Jesus.
3. Commit yourself to obedience to God.
4. Confess any known sins of yourself or your ancestors.
5. Forgive anyone who has ever hurt you.
6. Renounce all contact with occult or secret societies and get rid of all contact objects, books, jewelry, statues, etc.

7. Release yourself in the name of Jesus from the curse.

PRAYER OF RELEASE FOLLOWING AN ABORTION

In case you might have been involved with an abortion I would suggest that you add the following steps to your prayer of release. Pray out loud,

"I confess that having an abortion was murder and ask that You forgive me. I want to name the baby . . ."

Imagine yourself holding your unborn baby. Look at the baby and name it. Then say to the baby, "I can't bring you back, but I can come to you later."

Hold the baby up, present it to Jesus, and ask Him to care for your baby until you get to heaven. Then place the baby in a casket, close the lid, place a bouquet of flowers on the casket, and commit the baby into His care. By recognizing and identifying the baby you have put a closure to what you have done, and this will free you from the guilt and shame.

Now pray, "With the authority You have given me as a child of God, I release myself from every curse that has ever come upon me or affected me in any way. In the name of Jesus, amen."

CONTACT OBJECTS

One of the seven steps to freedom is to get rid of all contact objects. Many people do not know how to recognize a contact object.

Remember that demons are attracted to sight, sound and smell. Not only are demons attracted but they are also moved by sight, sound and smell. Those are the invitations they look for before they come in. They look for images that represent their kingdom — on posters, pictures, figurines, things that are unnatural (such as things with six hands and three heads). Don't burn Indian incense. The words in rock music attract demons. Don't keep jewelry or other items that would remind you of an old love affair. This keeps you soul-tied to that person.

ENFORCING GOD'S WORD AGAINST THE DEVIL

The Bible, speaking about Jesus, says in 1 Peter 2:24: "by whose stripes you were healed." If this is true, and it is, then it is illegal to be sick—in the same way it is illegal to be harassed by demons. The problem with the devil is that he is always operating in the illegal realm. He will try to instill sickness in you, even though the Bible says you are healed. He will send demons to harass you, even though it is illegal to be under a curse. Legally, Jesus has redeemed us from the curse. What we must do is learn to take the Word of God and enforce it against the works of the devil.

Legally, we have a right to break curses, based on Galatians 3:13: "Christ has redeemed us from the curse of the law, having become a curse for us." Jesus took the curse for us so that: "the blessing of Abraham might come upon the Gentiles in Christ Jesus, that we might receive the promise of the Spirit through faith" (v. 14). Notice the Bible says both the blessing and the promise of the Spirit come because of what Jesus did. As the curse is broken, greater sincerity comes in the believer because the Spirit of God moves more freely through that person.

An important principle is shown in Ephesians 6:12: "For we do not wrestle against flesh and blood, but against principalities, against powers, against the rulers of the darkness of this age, against spiritual hosts of wickedness in the heavenly places." Demons rule where there is darkness. Their authority comes where there is darkness. When light comes, as from revelation or knowledge, they no longer are in darkness and therefore they no longer have authority.

The Prayer of Loosing

Let's look for a moment at Mark 5:9, when Jesus was addressing the Gadarene demoniac: Jesus asked him, "What is your name?" And demoniac answered, "My name is Legion; for we are many." Jesus revealed a principle here. When He asked the name of the demon, the demons could no longer hide. When the demons could no longer hide, they lost their authority, and at the Word of Jesus, they had to come out. I feel this is the purpose of identifying the spirit in certain instances, so that it can no longer hide.

I want to show you how the devil works and teach you how to stop his attack. According to Matthew 12:43–45 we are told how a demon operates.

> When an unclean spirit goes out of a man, he goes through dry places, seeking rest, and finds none. Then he says, "I will return to my house from which I came." And when he comes, he finds it empty, swept, and put in order. Then he goes and takes with him seven other spirits more wicked than himself, and they enter and dwell there; and the last state of that man is worse than the first. So shall it also be with this wicked generation.

Now it looks like we are really in a mess. The demon has gone out, gathered seven of his friends stronger than himself, and entered back into our house. Seven is completion and eight is a new beginning. So the eight demons are starting over to wreak havoc in a life. How can we stop this from happening? We have authority over the devil, and Jesus equipped us to win the battle. The devil can't survive in an environment of truth. God's Word is truth. First, we are instructed to bind the strong man. "Or how can one enter a strong man's house and plunder his goods, unless he first binds the strong man? And then he will plunder his house" (Matt. 12:29).

How do you bind a strong man? Matthew 18:18 tells us: "Assuredly, I say to you, whatever you bind on earth will be bound in heaven, and whatever you loose on earth will be loosed in heaven." There are keys that bind and keys that loose. Whatever you forbid on earth is forbidden in heaven. Based on this biblical principle, I have written a sample prayer of loosing.

As we loose ourselves from curses, we can in turn glorify Jesus, and His name will be magnified. This is a prayer that I lead many times as I minister on breaking curses in people's lives. If you will pray this loosing prayer out loud, with sincerity in your heart, God will meet you at the point of your need and begin to set you free from curses that have harassed you for many years.

Father, in the name of Jesus and in Your authority I speak and say: "Satan by the power of the Word I bind you and command you to get out of my life. Get out of my family. Get out of my home. Get out of my finances. I declare that every family curse and every generational curse is broken and reversed in the name of Jesus."

I thank You for the authority You have given me, in the name of Jesus. Whatever I bind on earth is bound in heaven and whatever I loose on earth is loosed in heaven. I bind every spirit that would try to operate in my life, and I loose myself from every curse that has opened the door for the enemy to come in my life.

I loose myself from all curses of idolatry, witchcraft, or occultism.

I loose myself from all curses of death or destruction.

I loose myself from all curses of sickness or infirmity.

I loose myself from all curses of lust or perversion.

I loose myself from all curses of fear or torment.

I loose myself from all curses of pride or rebellion.

I loose myself from all curses of bondage and slavery.

I loose myself from all curses of poverty or lack.

I loose myself from all curses of divorce or separation.

I loose myself from all curses that would operate against my family.

I loose myself from any other curses that may be operating in my life to allow the enemy to come into my life.

I loose myself from these curses on both sides of my family back thirty generations and beyond. I take away the legal right the enemy has to operate in my life.

Lord, I thank You, that according to the Word of God, I can loose myself and I command every spirit that would hide in my life, you are being exposed. You will no longer be able to hide in the darkness, for the Holy Spirit is exposing you. You will leave my life, and I will be set free by the power of the Holy Spirit. I close every door that the enemy has in my life through a curse.

I thank You, Lord, for setting me free. I am redeemed from the curse of the law. The blessing of Abraham is upon my life. I receive the promise of the Spirit through faith. Thank You, Lord. No more sorrow, no more perversion, no more destruction can operate in my life because of a curse. I am blessed! I am blessed! I am blessed!

In Jesus' name, amen.

CHAPTER 9

....

Receive the Blessing

There is no doubt that Jesus made the provision for us to receive our blessing, just like He made the provision for us to receive salvation. We read in Galatians 3:13–14: "Christ has redeemed us from the curse of the law, having become a curse for us (for it is written, "Cursed is everyone who hangs on a tree"), that the blessing of Abraham might come upon the Gentiles in Christ Jesus, that we might receive the promise of the Spirit through faith."

The blessings of the Lord are a natural outpouring that He has set up for us. Still, we have to appropriate that provision and bring it to pass by agreeing with the provision He set up for us. Each thing we receive by having faith and overcoming doubt. Each of us must make that decision and then move in the decision we have made.

The first and foremost thing we must do to receive is make a decision! Don't let your tomorrows be consumed by feeding on yesterdays. The more we look backward, the less able we are to see forward. Every day we make decisions. Daily we are confronted with options. Our choices will either reflect faith or doubt. Some of the options we face are:

1. Being bitter vs. being better. Being bitter is an evil thing and therefore it is our choice to be better rather than being bitter. Many scriptures warn us not to be bitter. "Your own wickedness will correct you, and your backslidings will rebuke. Know therefore and see that it is an evil and bitter thing that you have forsaken the Lord your God" (Jer. 2:19).

2. Indifference vs. decisiveness. "Multitudes, multitudes in the valley of decision! For that day of the Lord is near in the valley of decision" (Joel 3:14). This is definitely not a time for indifference. The Lord is like a river, always flowing, and if we are not flowing with Him then we are going backward. The choice boils down to the fact that we are decisive and moving forward or we are going backward through default.

3. Lukewarmness vs. enthusiasm. "So then, because you are lukewarm, and neither hot nor cold, I will vomit you out of My mouth" (Rev. 3:16). There is no question in my mind but that God wants us on fire for Him. He tells us that we are to fan the flame of the gift that He has placed within us. Jeremiah testified of the fact that His Word was in Jeremiah's heart like a burning fire shut up in his bones.

4. Security vs. risk. We are told to go into all the world and preach the gospel, and to do that we will have to leave our security. The Bible tells us in Isaiah 54 that we are to enlarge the place of our tent and let them stretch out the curtains of our dwellings. We are told to not spare but rather to lengthen our cords and strengthen our stakes. This doesn't sound like security to me but it sounds like a risk. My choice is to follow the Word, regardless of the risk involved. How about you?

5. Coping with evil vs. overcoming evil. "Do not be overcome by evil, but overcome evil with good" (Rom. 12:2). Over and over the Bible tells us to do good and not evil. We are not to tolerate evil but instead dispel evil.

6. Resisting vs. receiving. It is always our choice to either resist or receive. When we stop resisting, we will receive. I personally don't believe it is possible to receive when you are resisting.

7. Choice vs. change. We have lots of choices in life, and it is up to us to make the decision to change. Once we have made a decision to change, then He is faithful to His promises to bring about the change in our lives. "The Lord Jesus will change our lowly body that it may be conformed to His glorious body, according to the working by which He is able even to subdue all things to Himself" (Phil. 3:21).

8. Peace vs. strife. "Mercy, peace, and love be multiplied to you" (Jude 2). We should resist strife and choose instead peace. Proverbs 17:14 offers great wisdom about avoiding strife: "The beginning of strife is like releasing water; therefore stop contention before a quarrel starts." The Bible says we are to stop it even before it starts.

9. Demanding more of others vs. demanding more of ourselves. The Bible instructs us to always return good for evil and make the right choice and not to demand of others. "…being reviled, we bless; being persecuted, we endure; being defamed, we entreat" (1 Cor. 4:12–13). We see in 1 Peter 3:8–9: "Finally, all of you be of one mind, having compassion for one another; love as brothers, be tenderhearted, be courteous; not returning evil for evil or reviling for reviling, but on the contrary blessing, knowing that you were called to this, that you may inherit a blessing."

10. Changing our lives by renewing our minds vs. staying in bondage. Romans 12:2: "And do not be conformed to this world, but be transformed by the renewing of your mind, that you may prove what is that good and acceptable and perfect will of God." We are told in Galatians 4:9 that we should never again desire to be in bondage! Our desire should be both to come out of bondage and to continually stay out of bondage.

THE BIGGEST OBSTACLE TO RECEIVING A BLESSING

I have found that the biggest obstacle in people receiving from God is that instead of receiving they are actually resisting. Of course, they don't realize they are resisting, but in fact they are. For example, many times when I lay hands on people and pray for them they will stagger backward instead of falling under the power. I asked God about this and He said it was because they were not receiving. If I ask individual people, they reply that they don't know why they stagger back and try to stay on their feet. Some think it is a reflex action.

I asked a man recently, "Why did you stagger back? Was it to get away from the power of God or was it because of fear of falling?"

"Oh, no," he replied. "I just don't want to give anyone a courtesy fall. I want it to truly be the power of God that knocks me down."

I replied, "Do you realize that the Holy Spirit is a gentleman and He does not force Himself on anyone? God gives us a choice. He will even allow us to go to hell if we refuse to bend to His will. We are the ones who have to make the decision. He gives us the power to accomplish His will, but He never overrides our will." I didn't tell him this, but I thought to myself that what he said

109

sounded like "spiritual pride." We should be extremely careful to avoid getting into "spiritual pride."

Another way of resisting instead of receiving is when people analyze just how God is moving. They use the excuse and say, "I want to be sure it is God. I don't want to get into deception." This motive sounds so good and pure, but let me ask you this: If you analyze everything God is doing and decide your mind can figure it out, then doesn't that make God the size of your mind? Would you like a God that was small enough to fit that mold? I don't know about you but I definitely want a GREAT BIG GOD! I certainly don't want to limit Him to my mind.

I recently heard a pastor's wife say to him, "You keep analyzing everything until you analyze the very life out of it." I truly think this is possible, and many times we analyze instead of just receiving what God is offering us. My prayer is that God would move in a mighty way upon every person who comes forward for prayer. His Word says that He wants to bless us, and I believe that is exactly what He wants to do.

As Stephen was about to be stoned, he warned the Jewish council about resisting the Holy Spirit: "You stiff-necked and uncircumcised in heart and ears! You always resist the Holy Spirit, as your fathers did, so do you" (Acts 7:48).

Stephen upbraided the council and the Jewish people for their unbelief. He said they made a habit of resisting the Holy Spirit. Do you think it is possible that when we do not receive from the Lord that He is as frustrated with us? I think that this is a strong possibility. Do you think we could be making a habit of resisting the Holy Spirit and be completely unaware of it? Do you think this could be an iniquity handed down through the generations? Do you think this could be our problem? I think that it is highly possible.

I have made it a habit recently when I pray for people and they stagger backward I do not chase after them. I go on to the next person for I feel they are resisting the Holy Spirit, and His anointing is too precious to be wasted. I feel that when they are ready and anxious to receive, then God will bountifully pour out His blessing upon them.

In 2 Corinthians 1:20, we read, "For no matter how many promises God has made, they are 'yes' in Christ. And so through Him the 'Amen' is spoken by us to the glory of God" (NIV).

Did you understand this scripture? All that is required of you is to agree with Jesus for these promises and they are yours. The receiving is up to you!

I have even heard some pastors say, "I have to be extremely careful. I don't want 'wildfire' to break out in my church." I have only one answer for that. If I were the pastor I would rather try to deal with wildfire than try to raise the dead. Some of our churches are resistant to the Holy Spirit that He has a most difficult time moving in their midst.

Recently, I was ministering to people and praying for them a young man stopped me and said, "I have great needs today and, I confess, I don't know how to receive. Could you help me?"

I smiled and said, "Thank God, for you are a likely candidate. The first thing you do is raise both hands in complete surrender to God. This is, in effect, saying to God, 'I give up. Do as You will to me!' The next thing is to close your eyes so you will not be aware of anything around you and can concentrate only on Him. Don't pray yourself, for you came to receive and you can't give out and receive at the same time. It is impossible to receive if you are praying and giving out. Close your mind on any doubt or unbelief or anything critical and open yourself to receive. Do not let your mind wander but concentrate on taking in and basking in His presence. Just as you would lie in the sun to get a tan, so you need to stay in His presence to get His blessings." After these simple instructions I prayed for him. He fell under the power of God, and the Lord did a mighty miracle in his life that day.

Sometimes when people fall under the power, they immediately scramble up and go their way. I urge them to stay in the presence of the Lord as long as possible. There is an awesome presence and anointing during prayer times such as this, and it behooves all of us to get everything God has for us. I feel that the longer we stay in His presence the greater the benefits will be.

THE RIGHT WAY TO RECEIVE

Some twenty years ago, when my husband and I were leading a weekly Bible study in a friend's home, we had a new couple visit. We met this likeable husband and wife for the first time as they came in the door. The husband seemed completely healthy, strong and robust. We took our chairs in a big circle, some thirty or thirty-five of us, but I kept looking at this new couple. Just before we started the teaching, I asked him to give us a word of testimony.

"I was wounded in the Korean War," he started. "Last week I went on a retreat with a local church group." (He gave the name of the church and the evangelist who was hosting the retreat and we were familiar with them).

"The evangelist called me forward with a word of knowledge and said the Lord wanted to heal me. He said I was crippled and on retirement, drawing social security and a pension as a disabled veteran. Well, the evangelist was right. I was unable to work and had been for a number of years. He prayed for me, and I was instantly healed and have been walking without aid ever since.

Before God healed me, I had to have crutches or be in a wheelchair to get around. Now look at me!"

A roar of joy went up from our group as we realized that this robust man had been a cripple only one week previous. After things quieted down some, he shared the reason he was attending our group. "All day today, I have been in severe pain. I thought I would come to this group and see if you would pray for me that I might get some relief."

My husband jumped up and said, "Yes. We will pray for you and God will take away the pain!" We gathered around him, laying hands on him, and prayed in faith. God touched him mightily, and he fell under the power and lay there on the floor. We all stood around for perhaps five minutes and he was still out, so we started our regular Bible study.

For about an hour we read and discussed Scripture, all the while our visitor lay in the middle of the circle, flat on his back, oblivious to anything going on around him. He was a study in receiving from God. He literally basked in the Lord's presence for an hour. As we finished our Bible study, he stirred and then sat up. A big grin came on his face and he testified to the fact there was no pain left. He later testified that never again did the pain return. It was the last stand the devil made trying to convince him that he was an invalid, but God convinced him he was healed.

Occasionally, we still see the couple, and more than twenty-five years later, he is still walking in divine health. They have continually served the Lord since that time. There was quite a stir when he went in and rescinded his disability pension and was able to walk with ease and do work he had been unable to do for years. There was no precedent for rescinding a disability pension, so the government had to do some paperwork they had not done before. They had never had an incident where a person placed on a disability pension had gotten healed and no longer needed the pension.

As I look back on this I believe that one of the major reasons he received his healing was because he was ready to receive without question. When he went under the power, he stayed under the power. He did not question whether it was the religious thing to do or not. He did not question whether my husband was an ordained minister or not. He did not question me as to my state of submission and my exact place in the body of Christ and whether I fit a certain mold. He just believed God and trusted Jesus to complete the job in his life. If we would come as he did, believing, we would receive.

Receiving from God is much less complicated than we make it out to be. Even little children know how to come to Jesus. "Then little children were brought to Him that He might put His hands on them and pray, but the disciples rebuked them. But Jesus said, 'Let the little children come to Me, and do not forbid them; for of such is the kingdom of heaven'"(Matt. 19:13–14). If we learned to receive like little children, our problems with receiving would end.

A year or so ago we were having some great services in our home church and I prayed for a little girl who was perhaps seven or eight years old. She immediately fell under the power and some twenty minutes later she still lay on the floor while her mother watched over her. Finally her father came up and said, "We need to go. I'll carry her to the car." So he took up the child and carried her to their van and they drove home.

All during this time she had not stirred and seemed to be in a trance. He carried her into the house and lay her on the sofa and again she did not rouse. After almost an hour she stirred. Her father had told the mother that she was asleep, but the mother was sure she was not. As the girl stirred, she told her mother the most amazing story.

"Jesus took me up to heaven, and it was so beautiful," she beamed. "There were flowers everywhere, and everything was clean, with the colors all so vivid that I loved it."

She continued, "I told Him that I wanted to live there for I loved Him very much," and then a frown came on her face.

"He said that I could not live there because I had never asked Him into my heart. I began to cry, and He said that everyone who lived in heaven had to ask Jesus to come into their heart and be born again. But I have known all about You since I was a small child," she told Him.

"But you have never asked Me to come and live in your heart," He gently reminded her.

"Then, will You come and live in my heart so I will be born again?" she entreated Him.

The answer was simple and direct, "Yes!"

This little girl received with simplicity. A great miracle was wrought in her life as she was born again. Some physical problems she was having at that time were healed also, but the real miracle was the new birth. Many times we think children don't know enough to move in the things of God, but because of their simple childlike faith, they move the heart of God!

CHAPTER 10

Freedom From Depression

Depression is a problem that commonly follows generational lines. Because so many people battle with depression, I want to encourage you through testimony and teaching that God will deliver you, even if you've been suffering for years. One of the first things God did for me and George after we were saved was to break the curse of depression that was over both of us. Since then, we have helped many others break free.

SYMPTOMS OF DEPRESSION

Webster's dictionary defines *depression* as "dejection, as of mind; gloominess, pressed down; downcast, discouraged and disheartened." Common symptoms of depression include feelings of sadness, hopelessness, helplessness, and worthlessness. People with depression experience difficulty sleeping and changes in appetite.

Sufferers no longer derive pleasure from activities that were once enjoyable, and they may have difficulty concentrating and making decisions. Depression also may be characterized by thoughts of death and suicide.

Depression not only affects your emotions, it also causes physical diseases. Some people have vague medical complaints such as aches and pains that won't go away, backaches, headaches, and stomach ailments. Chronically depressed people are at greater risk of developing cancer. Heart attack survivors who also have depression have an increased risk of dying within six months.

Blood tests can show the degree to which a person is suffering from depression. That's why it's so powerful to remember that when we receive Jesus, we receive His cleansing blood. Leviticus 17:11 tells us, "The life of the flesh is in the blood." When you receive Jesus as your Lord and Savior, you receive His cleansing blood. To receive Him, you confess with your mouth and believe in your heart that Christ was raised from the dead and you are then born again. At that moment you are adopted into the family of God and receive His DNA. The DNA in our blood is "the blueprint of our potential." The blood of Jesus enables you to fulfill all the destiny and purpose God has for your life.

In our natural bloodline we have family iniquities. Iniquities cause a bend in your nature toward certain conditions, for example, a bend toward good health, poor health, sound mind, or depression. What is a bloodline iniquity? An iniquity is a repeated sin pattern in your life, or a learned behavior pattern. For example, Uncle Joe always had depression around Christmas-time, and it became a family trait. Instead of rising above the family iniquity, we adopt a lethargic attitude toward that habit leads to hopelessness and discouragement. We think that we can never rise above the so-called "weaknesses" in our families.

The devil's job is to kill, steal and destroy. What better way to destroy you than to assign an army of demons that are familiar with your generation? This army of evil spirits is on assignment from Satan to destroy the plan and purpose that God has for you. But the good news is that Jesus has a plan for your life, and His plan is that you might have *life* and have it more abundantly. He wants you filled with joy, walking in peace, and living victorious and free from depression.

As you read these testimonies, remember that God is willing and able to meet your needs as well.

MY TESTIMONY

I was born in a small community in the foothills of Arkansas during the Depression years, when our nation struggling under a burden of poverty. Our family was struggling, much the same as many families during that time. We had no running water in our house, no inside bathrooms, no electric lights. In fact it was easier to list what we had than what we didn't have. Our "have" list was really short.

Recently I was meditating on just how far God has brought me, and I was awed with the revelation. During the past year I have been privileged to travel and minister in many parts of the United States, as well as foreign countries. It hardly seems possible that a little girl from the foothills of Arkansas could have traveled so far. Of course, the answer is that through the power of Jesus Christ, all things are possible.

I had female surgery at the age of thirty-two. Afterward, my hormones were extremely out of balance. I began to have drastic mood swings. I would be extremely happy,

118

functioning normally with my family and co-workers; and some small thing could go wrong and I would burst into tears, be depressed and just want to go to bed and sleep. There came a point that I did not want to be around people because I was afraid of the emotional outbursts. At this time I had only been a Christian three weeks. I believed healing was for others but not necessarily for me. I was ignorant of God's Word. My mind had not been renewed by the Word. So, when my doctor prescribed Valium for the "mood swings," I gladly took them. For six months I lived in a trancelike state of mind. I was fine until the Valium would almost wear off. But, I knew the next pill was coming and I could look forward to that.

We were on vacation in the Great Smoky Mountains of North Carolina. My husband took me and our two kids out to eat. It was time to take the Valium. I reached in my purse for the bottle of pills. They were not there. At that moment I literally fell apart. I panicked, became paranoid. I was too upset and unnerved to eat. My husband told the children to continue eating and he would take me to the motel, put me to bed, and be back to take care of them. He could not find the medicine. He gave me some pain-killer that I was taking that allowed me to sleep at night. There are no words to tell you how raw my nerves were at that time. I went into the deepest depression that I ever knew could be possible.

This was my wake-up call. The next day I bought a book called *Healing Through the Name of Jesus*. I began to study and meditate on the Word. I continued to take the Valium but was trying to cut down on the dose. I knew I was hooked on a prescription drug. I felt like Jesus was my real answer. I thought there had been a period of time that perhaps I needed the Valium, but it had now become a habit with which I could not deal.

God had miraculous delivered me from social drinking. Now I had traded one habit for another. Just as drinking had soothed my nerves and put me in a "don't care attitude," so had the Valium.

I started meditating on Psalm 103: "Bless the Lord, O my soul, And forget not all His benefits: Who forgives all your iniquities, who heals all your diseases, Who redeems your life from destruction, Who crowns you with lovingkindness and tender mercies, Who satisfies your mouth with good things, So that your youth is renewed like the eagle's. The Lord executes righteousness and justice for all who are oppressed." (This scripture spoke directly to me. It literally had my name on it.)

I knew then that I was oppressed by the devil. Through studying the Word I found out that my soul was my mind, my will, and my emotions. My mind was telling me that I needed the Valium. As my mind was being renewed by the Word the "mood swings" became less frequent.

When they did come, they were not as intense or severe and did not last as long. I was able to quote God's Word and encourage myself and to know that the Lord was freeing me daily. I had an increased desire to be free from the iniquity of depression. I did not want to be dependent on drugs. I wanted to be healed. My emotions were fighting my will and saying, "Without drugs you can't function." But God's Word said that He would redeem my life from destruction. He was satisfying my mouth with the good things from His Word, and the desire to use tranquilizers was decreasing daily. I set my will to come in line with what God said about me. He was executing righteousness and freeing me from oppression. I realized that since God was big enough to save me from sin, He was also powerful enough to deliver me from the iniquity in which I was now trapped.

The healing was a progression through the following:

120

Soul
mind
will emotions

1. Recognizing I had a problem.
2. Desiring not to be drug dependent.
3. Meditating on the Word (specifically, healing scriptures).
4. Realizing I had a new bloodline and that the life of God flowed in my veins.
5. I forgave everyone (even my ex-husband).

I had bitter root judgments against people. The Word of God changed my thinking. I stopped judging others and let God deal with my heart. At that point in my life I was still very angry at my ex-husband. During this time there was a court hearing over child support and custody. This really sent me into more dependence on the drug. Most depression is caused by anger turned inward. Bitter roots bear bitter fruits. We are told in Proverbs 23:7, "As a man thinks in his heart, so is he."

What are some of the steps to overcoming depression? Forgive everyone who has ever hurt and disappointed you. Thoughts of bitterness not only reflect in your countenance, but bitterness also causes you to experience medical problems. Bitterness dries the bones. (See Leviticus 17:11.) Since blood is produced in the bones, bitterness will rob you of your very life, because the life of the body is in the blood.

Ephesians 4:23 says: "Be renewed in the attitude of your mind" (NIV). Your attitude will dictate your actions. As my mind was renewed, so were my actions. Depression and dependence on drugs stopped being a part of those actions.

One day I decided to flush all the pills down the commode. That was twenty-seven years ago, and I have not had any mood-altering drugs since then. I am free by the name of Jesus, set free through His blood and healed by His stripes.

Getting Free

I suffered for many years with bouts of depression so debilitating that I was convinced there was no way I could be set free. In fact, in 1969, before Mary Jo and I were married, I asked her if she could possibly survive my bouts of depression. She had never seen me in the pits I was prone to descend into, for most of our courtship had been exhilarating and uplifting. Still, I knew that sooner or later the depression would return, and I wanted her to be aware of it. She assured me that she could deal with it, so in June we were married. If she had known how bad my depressions got, I wonder if she would have been so sure she could deal with it.

Sure enough, after only a few weeks of wedded bliss, the first session of depression came on me. I went into the bedroom, sat on the floor with my trusty Gibson guitar, and began to pick out depressing country music. When depression came, that had always been my habit, and I was continuing true to form. Mary Jo tried to break the depression. When that tactic failed, she did the next best thing— she ignored me. That was hard to do for I was right in her way each time she came into the bedroom, but she managed to step over me and go on with things. After about twelve hours of this, I came out of it and returned to my former self. It seemed as if there was nothing in particular that triggered a bout of depression — it just happened.

Our marriage was most gratifying to both of us, and we were sailing along through life with only minor problems (although the depression was certainly not minor). As months went by, the bouts of depression grew further and further apart, but when they did come, they were rough. Then, after about two years of marriage, we started going to church and received Jesus as Lord and

122

Savior. A new life was underway, and we were both hungry for the Word and for what God could do in our lives. As I look back on it now, I am so thankful that He instructed me and sent worthy servants to help me find the way to set us both free in so many areas of our lives.

I can look back now in retrospect and realize just how I kicked the habit of depression. Praise God! There were three things that had me bound, and I now realize that all three had to be broken in my life for me to enjoy the freedom that I now do. First, there was iniquity (or a bend in my nature) that was handed down from my Grandfather Clouse, for he also had fits of depression. I was a small boy when he died, so I didn't see his depression firsthand, but my older sister did and she told me about him and the things he said and did. That iniquity had to be uprooted and expelled from my life before I could get any measure of relief from depression.

Second, my mind had to be renewed, according to the Word of God and not according to the way the world thinks. Ephesians 4:23 says: "Be renewed in the attitude of your mind" (NIV). God, through the ministry of a dear brother, gave me some pointers on renewing my mind and attitude. I had some 3-by-5-inch cards that instructed me exactly what to do. You will find this laid out in detail further in this book. They instructed me on how to make good thoughts become habit forming. These habits changed my attitude, which changed my thinking from negative to positive. My actions also became positive as well as my behavior. As my mind was renewed, so were my actions (and depression was no longer a part of those actions).

Third, and most important, is that we must rely on the Lord Jesus to intercede on our behalf, and set us free. Today, as I look back on my life and repeated fits of depression prior to 1971, I am amazed that I survived all those years. My life today is so fulfilling it is hard to remember that other life. Praise God that Mary Jo had enough fortitude to see me through that most difficult time, and the Lord Jesus came to my rescue and plucked me out of the miry clay!

FREED FROM THREE YEARS OF DEPRESSION

Sylvia Davenport, my good friend and board member of CRM and Intercessor, who travels with me whenever she can. Sylvia wrote down this testimony for us about freedom from depression.

In September of 1976, after three year of deep depression, I found the one and only true cure — Jesus!

After a total hysterectomy at the age of thirty, and being given no hormone replacement, I was trapped on a perpetual emotional roller coaster. I became a crying, sad and nagging wife. Depression nearly cost me everything. Doctors gave me tranquilizers and a prescription mood elevator. These turned me into a zombie! I was so medicated I could not function.

When in depression, it was horrible. There were days I did not go out of the house. I would sit and dwell on my problems. My mind felt as if there were a dome of heavy, dark bricks on it.

I went to a Christian psychologist who suggested that I be examined by a gynecologist. I found a good doctor who did blood work and discovered I had a hormone imbalance. He prescribed hormones and a mild tranquilizer. I began to function better mentally but still had depression bouts. This all took place over a two-year period. During this time my marriage nearly fell apart; I was suicidal, and I only weighed eighty-nine pounds.

A friend led me to Jesus. I was told to read the Book of Philippians two times a day for four weeks. I did this faithfully, for I was told it would cause a change in my life. How true it was! In three months my husband, Gene, saw such a change in me I led him to the Lord. I then began to confess God's Word by reading from a list of scriptures out loud three times a day.

I had been accustomed to taking medication regularly. So, instead of taking tranquilizers, I quoted the Word regularly. Quoting and reading the Word aloud, my husband praying with me daily, and some Christian counseling at church, was the beginning of deep healing for me. After a period of renewing my mind with the Word, the counselor prayed deliverance for me and I was totally free from depression. When I went through deliverance I felt the heaviness lift from my head. I felt light for the first time in years and totally free from depression. That has been over twenty-five years now, and I am still free. All praise goes to Jesus. He is the answer.

Part 3

Benefits
of
Forgiveness

CHAPTER 11

I Had to Forgive in My Own Family

More people are held in bondage due to the direct influence of unforgiveness than any other way. One of the most important truths we can learn when we become Christians is the truth and power in forgiveness! As we forgive, a release and a freedom come in our lives that cannot come any other way.

One of the greatest lessons on forgiveness is in Matthew 18 about a servant whose master forgave a huge debt. This same servant in turn refused to forgive a fellow servant a measly little debt, and the master had him thrown into prison for his lack of compassion. I hope you will examine your own life as we look at this scripture and the implications contained therein. Because God forgave us, we can forgive others *even if they don't deserve forgiveness.*

But first, let's look at what Jesus said in John 20:23: "If you forgive the sins of any, they are forgiven them, if you retain the sins of any, they are retained." The first time I read this verse I was stunned. Did this really mean that if I did not forgive people they would be in bondage and likewise if they did not forgive me then I would be in bondage? This was a completely new concept to me, and I began to research the Word to see if I understood the verse correctly.

Then I discovered Jesus' parable in Matthew 18:23–27:

> Therefore the kingdom of heaven is like a certain king who wanted to settle accounts with his servants. And when he had begun to settle accounts, one was brought to him who owed him ten thousand talents. But as he was not able to pay, his master commanded that he be sold, with his wife and children and all that he had, and that payment be made. The servant therefore fell down before him, saying, "Master, have patience with me, and I will pay you all!" Then the master of that servant was moved with compassion, released him, and forgave him the debt."

At today's prices, the value of a talent of silver is about $1,950, which means his debt totaled about two million dollars. Now, after the king forgave his debt, this servant was a free man. Free! Can you relate to this? Have you at some time in your life been set free by the Lord and, yet, due to some silly thing you did, you put yourself right back in bondage? Now, let's continue reading in verse 28 and see what happened next in this story as Jesus related it.

> But that servant went out and found one of his fellow servants who owed him a hundred denarii, and he laid hands on him and took him by the

throat, saying, 'Pay me what you owe!' So his fellow servant fell down at his feet and begged him, saying, 'Have patience with me, and I will pay you all.' And he would not but went and threw him into prison till he should pay the debt."

A man whose master had forgiven him a debt of some two million dollars had starting choking his fellow servant to get a mere seventeen dollars. Then, after choking him, he had him thrown into prison for nonpayment of the debt. Isn't that a sad picture? It's a sad fact that many people react this way in the world in which we live today. But God has a better plan for our lives if we will only follow His guidance.

Let's continue reading in verse 31. *till we*

we will be in bondage *forgive,*

So when his fellow servants saw what had been done, they were very grieved, and came and told their master all that had been done. Then his master, after he had called him, said to him, "You wicked servant! I forgave you all that debt because you begged me. Should you not also have had compassion on your fellow servant, just as I had pity on you?" And his master was angry, and delivered him to the torturers until he should pay all that was due to him. So My heavenly Father also will do to you if each of you, from his heart does not forgive his brother his trespasses.

Remember, this was Jesus teaching and He said that the heavenly Father would put us in prison (or bondage) if we put others in bondage. In today's world many people are seeking deliverance, and rightfully so, but many are in bondage and cannot get set free simply because of unforgiveness. Jesus said "his master was angry, and delivered him to the torturers . . ." Think on that for a minute. Do you suppose that Jesus meant that we would be turned over to the devil (torturer) if we refused to forgive? If He turns us over to the torturers, do you think we can get deliverance without forgiving? I think not!

Jesus chose his twelve disciples and sent them out in His power and authority and told them in Matthew 10:8, "Freely you have received, freely give." I think that because we, in the body of Christ, have received forgiveness for all our sins by the Father in heaven, that, in the same way, we must forgive everyone, regardless of the offense. "But you don't know what that person did to me," you may say. It really doesn't matter what was done. The Word does not say we must forgive if the person deserves to be forgiven. The Word simply says, *forgive!*

The day that Jesus hung on the cross, He looked down and said, "Father, forgive them, for they do not know what they do" (Luke 23:34). Who do you think was right in that situation? The only person that was right was Jesus, and yet, He was the one who forgave them. Do you get the message? Jesus forgave them, and now it is up to us. We are the only ones who can retain sin against someone else. It is time we started dealing with what God says about forgiveness and relationships and get in obedience to His Word.

I know that it is hard to do what the Lord asks. I was dealing with a brother one day who had many problems. When I shared with him about forgiveness he said, "But, I don't want to do that. If I do that, it will change my personality and I will be another person."

I looked him squarely in the eye and replied: "If you expect to get victory with God you are going to have to change and be another person. "If you want victory in

131

your life, you must walk in obedience to the Lord. The Word states that "if we abide in Him and His Word abides in us, then we will know the truth and the truth will set us free" (John 8:32). When we start realizing that the truth really will set us free, we will be willing to do what God asks.

A RELIGION OF RIGHT RELATIONSHIP

I have come to realize that it makes no difference whatsoever who was right and who was wrong in causing unforgiveness. The only one you need to be right with is God Himself. When you are right with Him, then you in turn are right with your brother or sister. Your relationship horizontally is the same as your relationship vertically. Your relationship with your heavenly Father is a reflection of your relationship with the people you are associated with. In 1 John 4:20, we read, "If someone says, 'I love God,' and hates his brother, he is a liar . . ." Those are strong words, but they are God's words! Meditate on that!

Jesus was our example in forgiveness. We must follow His example and forgive freely, just as He did, regardless of who is at fault. Let's look at another example of His teaching in the Sermon on the Mount: "Therefore if you bring your gift to the altar, and there remember that your brother has something against you, leave your gift there before the altar, and go your way. First be reconciled to your brother, and then come and offer your gift" (Matt. 5:23), Jesus said, "If you remember that your brother has something against you . . ." Don't think about who wronged you; focus on whether others feel that you have wronged them!

Many times we think that Christianity is a religion of right doctrine, when in reality, it is a religion of right relationship. The Bible says we are to go our way and be reconciled, then come to the altar and praise God when we are free! Then we are not only free, but we in turn release our brother. Hallelujah! In the process of going to your brother you not only release him, but you also release yourself as well.

Some years ago my husband and I had a falling out with a brother in the Lord who was a pastor. We were closely associated with him in ministry but felt a direct leading from the Lord to attend another church. This brother's church was some distance from our home, and we had been there for about a year when the Lord impressed upon us that we were to leave. When we told him that we felt we were to attend another church he did not agree with our decision. He became rather ugly about the situation, but we stayed firm in our decision and refused to take offense. God had been teaching us about forgiveness, and we in turn blessed him and his family with a gift of the entire Bible on tape. That was an impressive gift at that time. Did my flesh feel like giving him a gift? No! But God impressed us to do it and because of that we, as well as our brother, were set free.

It all came down to what we did with the situation. It wasn't a matter of whether he was innocent of wrong-doing or whether we were innocent of wrongdoing. What did matter was that we forgave him. We do not have to prove that we are right; we only have to prove that we are willing to forgive.

Jesus taught His disciples to pray: "And forgive us our debts, as we forgive our debtors" (Matt. 6:12). This teaching was at the heart of what we now call The Lord's Prayer. Then He explained why it was so important to forgive others: "For if you forgive men their trespasses, your heavenly Father will also forgive you. But if you do not forgive men their trespasses, neither will your Father forgive your trespasses" (Matt. 6:14–15). No matter how hard I try, I'm sure, at some time, I will do something to my brother or sister that I should not. Likewise, at some time and in some instance, they in turn will trespass against me. Jesus says that if I don't forgive them, then the Father won't forgive me! That's heavy. It seems that I don't have a choice. I must forgive! And I will continue to pray that they too will forgive me, so we may both be free!

LOVE, DO GOOD, BLESS, AND PRAY

Jesus gave another powerful teaching about how to treat an enemy in Luke 6:27–28: "But I say to you who hear: Love your enemies, do good to those who hate you, bless those who curse you, and pray for those who spitefully use you." Jesus gave us four directives here. He said to love them, do good to them, bless them and pray for them. It's time that we Christians learn to do these four things instead of holding others in unforgiveness.

God dealt with me in a most powerful way concerning this scripture. Some years ago my husband and I attended a prayer meeting being led by an evangelist. There was singing and sharing, and we both enjoyed it tremendously. Then the evangelist asked if anyone wanted individual prayer, and we both went forward, for we were hungry for God. Through the word of knowledge, the evangelist asked me, "Who do you need to forgive?"

I responded, "No one."

"How about your ex-husband?" The thought of forgiving him infuriated me, for he had left me with two small children. I had thought I had forgiven him, but as the anger welled up in me, I knew I had not. He was truly my enemy, and I did not want to forgive him. I managed to choke out the words, "I forgive him," and hot tears

rushed down my cheeks. As I was loosed from the unforgiveness, I was slain in the Spirit, and a new and lasting
peace swept over me.

My husband was in much the same shape that I was.
His ex-wife was also a bone of contention for him. He, at
his turn, forgave her, and he too was slain in the Spirit
and experienced that same cleansing peace. After forgiving our previous mates, in the ensuing weeks, we
followed the instructions Jesus gave in His Word. We
began to do good to them. I even gave some clothes to
my ex-husband's new wife, because she needed them
badly. When that happened, I knew I had truly forgiven.
We began to bless them, and most of all we began to pray
for them. Within a six-month span, both of our ex-mates
were saved and started attending church. God's Word
will work in our lives if we will only give it a chance.

To him who strikes you on the one cheek, offer
the other also. And from him who takes away your
cloak, do not withhold your tunic either. Give to
everyone who asks of you. And from him who
takes away your goods do not ask them back. And
just as you want men to do to you, you also do to
them likewise. But if you love those who love
you, what credit is that to you? For even sinners
love those who love those who love them. And if
you do good to those who do good to you, what
credit is that to you? For even sinners do the same.
And if you lend to those from whom you hope to
receive back, what credit is that to you? For even
sinners lend to sinners to receive as much back.
But love your enemies, do good, and lend, hoping
for nothing in return, and your reward will be
great, and you will be sons of the Most High. For
He is kind to the unthankful and evil. Therefore be

> merciful, just as your Father also is merciful.
> —MATTHEW 6:29–36

When one of my friends heard this teaching for the first time, she immediately felt conviction because she was constantly grumbling about people who borrowed her books and were slow about returning them. As conviction hit her, she bowed her head and asked God to forgive her for complaining. She also stated, "I forgive each person who at anytime has failed to return anything borrowed, regardless of what it was or when it was. Amen." She felt peace flood her soul, and she was sure she was free of the feelings.

The thing she did not expect began to happen almost immediately. People began to walk up and hand her books, tapes, and various other items they had borrowed in times past. Much to her surprise, not only did the prayer set her free, that same prayer also released all the others as well, who in turn brought back a flood of things that had been borrowed. What an exciting concept! Verse 37 sums it all up: "Judge not, and you shall not be judged. Condemn not, and you shall not be condemned. Forgive, and you will be forgiven!"

JUDGE NOT, CONDEMN NOT, AND FORGIVE

My husband and I really had to zero in on Luke 6:37 in our own families—judge not, condemn not, and forgive. George did not get saved until after he had raised his three children. He had raised them outside the church, and we immediately began to pray that they and their mates would receive the Lord. His two daughters and their husbands were born again, and then the whole family united together to bring about salvation for his oldest son. We read in Matthew 18:19: "Again I say to you that if two of you agree on earth concerning anything that they ask, it will be done for them by the Father in heaven." This was what Jesus said, so we relied on that word and we all agreed together.

He was quite rebellious, rode a chopper motorcycle, and did many things he should not have done. George, of course, had previously judged him, condemned him and constantly spoke bad of him. As we got the revelation of forgiveness, we stopped judging, we stopped condemning, and we forgave and began to love him, do good to him, bless him, and pray for him. Again, God was true to His Word, for within a couple of months he too was saved!

I, too, began to see my family in a different light. I had always felt that my mother and father had not wanted another child when I was born. It was Depression years, and there were four other children already in the family. There was hardly enough food to go around. I, through rebellion, had left home in my teen years, thinking they would be better off with me gone. They, in turn, felt condemnation due to the fact they could not supply the needs of a teenage girl.

As Luke 6:37 burned in my heart, I went to my parents and asked them to forgive me for being a rebellious daughter. What a surprise I got as they both cried and insisted it was their fault, for they did not know how to deal with the hard times. I discovered that none of us were wrong in that particular situation. Through misunderstanding and refusing to talk it out and forgive we had wasted many years that we could have all been more closely related and much happier. It seems such a shame that it took so many years for me to forgive and bring forgiveness that brought about such miraculous freedom. The last few years of my parents' lives we truly enjoyed each other because of the truth of the Word. Anytime we were together we were excited and fellowshipped greatly.

Getting Free

My parents lived in Arkansas and we lived in Florida, but we kept in close touch through the telephone. Mom called me one day and said she had not slept well the night before due to a small group of young men who had gathered outside her house under the street light and talked and laughed most of the night. They had been doing this several times a week, and she was greatly agitated by it. She even called the police a couple of times. Each time the group left before the police arrived, so the police had been unable to get anything settled. The Lord immediately reminded me of Luke 6:37. I told Mom that she needed to forgive them and loose them. Mom certainly wasn't too enthusiastic about that idea, but she agreed to do it anyway.

Would you believe that the problem was solved?

After she prayed and forgave them, they immediately changed their habit patterns, and the very next week one person in the group was saved. Mom became a real believer in the power of forgiveness. She not only forgave them, she began to do good to them, to bless them and pray for them. She didn't know each individual name, but the names she did know, she spoke out and the rest she asked the Lord to bless them as well. What a great difference it made in her life, as well as changing their lives, too.

The lessons on forgiveness were the way that God introduced me to the truths behind getting free from bondage. Of all the root causes of curses, unwillingness to forgive is the most common. More people are held in bondage due to the direct influence of unforgiveness than any other way. In the next four chapters you will see how to forgive so that you will experience: Prosperity, Restoration of Marriage, Healing, Unity in Relationships.

no forgiveness
A) sensitive
B) personal

138

CHAPTER 12

....

Forgiveness Brings Prosperity

With most of us, the problem with unforgiveness comes about because of our flesh. We are offended and feel that we are perfectly justified in the way we feel and therefore refuse to forgive. If we look at Isaiah 40:6b–8, God defines just what is important: "All flesh is grass, and all its loveliness is like the flower of the field. The grass withers, the flower fades, because the breath of the Lord blows upon it; surely the people are grass. The grass withers, the flower fades, but the word of our God stands forever." Our flesh says we are hurt and we refuse to forgive. God's Word stands forever! He says we must forgive. It is time we in the body of Christ settle this issue once and for all.

In the same way we are to settle the issue about prosperity. Paul taught in 2 Corinthians 8:9, "For you know the grace of our Lord Jesus Christ, that though He was rich, yet for your sakes He became poor, that you through

His poverty might become rich." Jesus made the provision by going to the cross, but it is up to each of us to walk in faith and bring about His provisions.

As we look in the Old Testament, I find that the most complete word on prosperity comes from Joshua 1:8: "This Book of the Law shall not depart from your mouth, but you shall meditate in it day and night, that you may observe to do according to all that is written in it. For then you will make your way prosperous, and then you will have good success." I have no doubts that God intends for us to do just what this scripture says. We must read the Bible, meditate on the Bible, talk about the Bible, observe everything written in the Bible, do everything the Bible tells us to do . . . and then . . . our way will be prosperous!

Several years ago we were close friends with a couple who were about our age. I will call them Bill and Lisa (not their correct names) for the sake of telling the story. We were closely related to them in our church at the time and fellowshipped on a regular basis. They came to us and asked for help with a trying problem in their life. Their bills had piled up until it seemed they were insurmountable. They loved the Lord, were trying desperately to walk in His pathways, believed they should be walking in prosperity, but it just seemed like they could not make ends meet financially. They both had good jobs and made good money, but still things just would not balance.

My husband and I talked with them and decided that we would have a meeting at their house the following week. My husband asked them to have all their bills on the table, and we would go through them and pray over them. They were very receptive, and at the appointed day they had prepared everything the way we had asked. The four of us gathered around the dining room table, where all the bills were laid out, and began to pray. We asked

God to show us exactly how He wanted to handle the situation.

As we started looking at the statements of bills, we were staggered. There were credit card bills, department store bills, drug store bills, furniture store bills, power bills, telephone bills, rent bills, and on and on. Bill had taken the time to add them all up, and it was a five-figure total. It seemed that no one could get in that much financial trouble. The first thing my husband looked at was the power bill, and it was several hundred dollars. In Florida it's hot, so the air conditioning was running almost all the time, and it seemed that almost every light in the house was on. They had two teenage children, and they were constantly going in and out of the house, leaving the doors standing open with the air conditioner laboring. We suggested that they turn off the lights whenever they left a room, and that they close the doors behind them when they went outside. "What difference will that make?" Lisa interjected. "That's such a small thing, in comparison to the total." We assured her that these were indeed small steps, but God expects us to do our part and then He will do His part.

We then led them outside to the power meter and laid hands on it and asked God to take all waste out. They truly needed electrical power, but their bills were much too high. Of course, their power meter was right by the side of the road so that everyone could see the four of us laying hands on it and praying. Jesus said in Luke 9:26, "For whoever is ashamed of Me and My Words, of him the Son of Man will be ashamed when He comes in His own glory, and in His Father's, and of the holy angels." We were not ashamed, and we prayed fervently. What a sight that must have been—the four of us with our heads bowed and our hands on the power meter as a steady stream of cars drove by.

Then we went back into the house and anointed each doorway with oil and prayed over them that God would provide all their needs but then in turn take out all the waste. Suddenly the Lord impressed a question upon me, and I immediately asked Lisa, "Do you have unforgiveness toward someone?" She admitted that she did—toward her ex-husband. He had deserted her and her two children and had left her with a mountain of bills. "He's a snake-in-the-grass!" she blasted. She and Bill had been married only about two years and had been unable to get bills caught up. In fact, they were getting further in debt each day. That was the reason they so desperately needed help.

I ministered to Lisa about the importance of forgiveness, and she immediately got the revelation. With tears streaming she forgave him and asked God to forgive her. Then she prayed and blessed him, wherever he was. Bill also did his share of forgiving and repenting. You could feel the electricity in the air as the power of the Holy Spirit permeated that small dining area. After the prayers of forgiveness, we laid hands on the pile of bills and asked God to do a miracle and eliminate them. Then we asked Bill to total the bills each month and make a tangible note each time he could see God working. Meanwhile, they would work diligently to lower the balance. They were each to do their part in turning off lights, resisting sales, and making a conscience effort to get out of debt.

At the end of the first month, Bill came rushing into our weekly prayer meeting, very excited. "I can hardly believe it," he exclaimed. "I totaled up the bills and it comes up to almost two thousand dollars less than it was last month. How could that be? I didn't think we had paid that much! And besides that, our power bill just came in today, and it was half what it was last month."

We all shared in his excitement and right then and there decided that God is capable of doing things the way He wishes, whether we can figure it out or not. In fact, I concluded that my brain couldn't figure out God, and even if it could, that would make God no bigger than my brain, and I certainly didn't want that!

Each week during our prayer meeting, Bill and Lisa shared about what God was doing. What a blessing that was to each of us. As the months went by each of the individual debts were settled. After a year's time they announced they were all paid. Many times I have thought about each of them forgiving. They had earnestly tried to walk in God's blessing but had been unsuccessful due to unforgiveness. Once that bondage was broken off them, the blessings followed. They discovered 2 Corinthians 9:6–8: "But this I say: He who sows sparingly will also reap sparingly and he who sows bountifully [or, with blessings, as the Amplified Bible states] will also reap bountifully [or, with blessings]. So let each one give as he purposes in his heart, not grudgingly or of necessity; for God loves a cheerful giver. And God is able to make all grace abound toward you, that you, always having all sufficiency in all things, may have an abundance for every good work." They now found, with God's blessings on their finances instead of the curses of unforgiveness, this scripture was really true.

With all the credit cards and other bills paid off they were able to buy a home instead of renting, which they were doing at that time. Then they, in turn, started to have prayer meetings in their home and move in the power of the ministry God had called them to. About a year later they started a church, and God has continued His blessing in their lives. That is proof positive in the power of obeying God, forgiving everyone, and releasing people from bondage.

143

CHAPTER 13

······································

Forgiveness Heals Marriages

When someone does us wrong, we feel as though they have taken something that belonged to us away—regardless of what it might have been. It could be peace, happiness, joy, or something tangible, and now they owe it to us. When we are in unforgiveness, that means we are going to hold them accountable for whatever we think they have taken from us. This is foremost with people who are having marriage problems. In Ephesians 4:32, we read: "Be kind to one another, tenderhearted, forgiving one another, even as God in Christ forgave you." Since God did forgive us, then we likewise should forgive anyone who wrongs us.

I found this to be true with some very good friends some years ago. This couple—I shall call them John and Pauline—were drawn to my husband and me, but there seemed to be some sort of strife between them. Each of them were sweet in their own way. We both liked them, but there was that underlying spirit that came out now and then. Finally, we sat down to talk to them and try to get to the root of the problem.

They had been married for thirty-four years and had two children who were each married with children of their own and living in another part of the country. We prayed for John first, and he was slain in the Spirit and broke out into laughter as he lay on the floor. Pauline confided that it was the first time she had heard him laugh in years. What a waste of years!

Then it came time for Pauline. She began her story of hurts, disappointments, resentment and a massive accumulation of unforgiveness. Tears flowed freely as she forgave and then forgave some more. As the Lord dealt with them both, we prayed for them and could literally see the depression lift. John said they had stayed together through the years purely out of a sense of duty that they should. We continued to pry to get to the very root of their problems.

They had finally gotten saved and knew the Lord, but there was very little change in their marriage. Then Pauline had to have female surgery, which, in turn, left her cold and indifferent to anything intimate with her mate. John confided that this had put a strain on their already badly strained marriage. God had delivered him from smoking and drinking at his salvation, so he asked Him to also deliver him from sexual desires. God did just that, so the marriage had continued on that rocky road, with very little fulfillment for either of them.

At the gentle urging of the Holy Spirit, I felt that this was the time to pray. We urged each of them to forgive the other for all the years they felt they had wasted. Each wanted their lives to be happier and more fulfilled, they just didn't know how to go about getting the job done. John forgave Pauline for each and every time he had felt resentment, and she in turn forgave him for all the hurts and disappointments. The power of God was upon both of them as they began to break free of the bondage they had been walking in. They left that night with a new resolve to love each other completely without reservations. As they went home, arm in arm, we blessed them.

John later told us what transpired. They went home and went to bed as usual, in separate twin beds. The next morning Pauline felt depressed, so they knelt by their beds and prayed together to start the day. Later that day, she said, "I promised God last night that I would do all in my power to fulfill my marital obligations as a wife and prayed that we could again enjoy intimacy as we had years ago." John admitted that since he had prayed that the Lord would take away sexual desire he had serious doubts about being able to perform. Still, he felt he should trust God, so he prayed that God would again awaken his desires.

As they knelt by the bed that night to pray, each of them began to laugh uncontrollably, and God healed that marriage. My husband and I still know this couple, and their marriage remains strong and vibrant. What a blessing forgiveness is! A marriage that was a marriage in name only became a beautiful testimony to the Lord!

You always have a choice whether you want to forgive or not. Forgiveness is a decision. Unforgiveness is a sin! Psalm 66:18 says: "If I regard iniquity in my heart, the Lord will not hear." This means that if I don't have iniquity, then He will hear. That's what happens when husbands and wives forgive each other.

LETTING GO OF THE PAST

My husband and I have dealt with couples in our church who have needed counseling, and many times it is only a matter of talking things out and getting the lines of communications open. Other times there are issues that run much deeper. Usually these issues are centered around forgiveness, or, to put it bluntly, *un*forgiveness on the part of one or both spouses. We were good friends with one such couple. They seemed fairly happy most of the time, but occasionally they had a flare up that was unexplainable. They asked if they could come over to our house and discuss some issues and we invited them over.

The four of us sat down and immediately started prodding for the root of the problem. I am a confronter by nature, and I feel that the quicker you uncover the problem, the sooner you will find the solution. Jim and Rita (not their true names) had both been married before. Jim was divorced with two children from a previous marriage, and Rita was a widow, also with two children. We knew, from past experience, that a situation like this would create many opportunities for unforgiveness in each person's life. I began to question each about how they felt about the other's children, previous mates, etc. Much to my surprise, there seemed to be no problem there. My husband and I looked at each other with questioning eyes as to which way to go at this point. We stopped and prayed for the Holy Spirit to guide us so we would not waste time but would instead get to the root of the problem.

"What seems to cause you two to disagree?" I asked Rita.

"One thing is because he is so sloppy," she blurted out. "Every time we start to go to church I ask him which tie and coat he is wearing, and he replies, 'None,' and that starts it. He knows I do not like him to go to church sloppy. I try to get him to go to the shopping center to buy a new suit and he refuses."

"I don't want a new suit," he shot back. "I don't even

want to wear the sports coat I have now."

I was appalled at the viciousness of their exchange.

"Don't you love him anymore?" I asked Rita.

"He is repulsive to me," she literally spat out the words.

My husband later told me that he lost hope at that point. He felt those words were so harsh and vindictive and hurtful that we would have a most difficult time bringing them into agreement of any kind at this session. He said he was ready to call it off and wait for another day, but God prodded me to dig a little deeper.

"Why don't you want to wear a coat and tie?" I asked Jim, searching for something to rescue our discussion.

"I don't know," Jim answered matter-of-factly. "I guess it all goes back to my mother always wanting me to dress up and go to church."

"So, what's wrong with that?" I continued my quest.

"I didn't want to do it for she was such a hypocrite," Jim's voice broke as he said it. After perhaps a minute, as we remained quiet, he continued. "I was about five years old when my father and mother got in an argument on Sunday morning as she was preparing breakfast. He said something she didn't like and she turned around and hit him in the head with the iron frying pan. He was bleeding pretty bad, so they called the ambulance and took him to the hospital. After they left with him, she made me put on my coat and tie and go to church. I was furious because my daddy was hurt bad, and she wanted me to go to church with a coat and tie." At this point he broke into tears.

"Oh, my poor darling," Rita said, as she put her arms around him. (This is the same lady who said, "You are repulsive to me," only a few minutes before.) The next five minutes were spent with her rocking him in her arms and him sobbing at the remembrance of the hurt.

After a few minutes, we settled down and analyzed the whole situation. Jim had never thought about what made him so mad every time Rita mentioned him getting dressed for church. We carefully led him in a prayer for forgiveness for his mom and his dad as well. Then we led Rita in a prayer of repentance for all the times she had harassed him. What a time of freedom resulted from that!

Psalm 78:38 speaks of God's mercy: "But He, being full of compassion, forgave their iniquity, and did not destroy them." Jim's iniquity (bend in his nature) had been there for many years, and he did not even understand where it was coming from. Even so, when the iniquity was brought to light and Jim forgave his mother, then forgiveness came through Rita as well, and their marriage was healed. The very next day they went to the shopping center and bought Jim a new suit and on Sunday morning he proudly wore it to church. Not only that, but it has been over five years since this incident, and they testify that their marriage is happier than it has ever been because of the power of forgiveness.

Chapter 14

Forgiveness Brings Healing

We must always remember that forgiveness involves three parties. First, forgiveness concerns the other person. Second, forgiveness is closely related with God, who is ultimately the creditor, or the one to whom all debts are owed. Third, forgiveness causes changes in us. When we release others from their debts, we in turn, release ourselves from the painful effects they had on us. When we harbor bitterness against others, that bitterness eats away at us. The only way to get that poison out of our system is by forgiving others.

REJECTION

About three years ago, at the *Charisma* Women's Conference, I was teaching a workshop concerned with breaking generational curses off your life. At the end of the session, after I had prayed a prayer of release, this one lady came up and said, "I still have multiple problems." She had glasses with very thick lens that were very dark and curved around the side of her face. She said she had an inherited eye disorder that was getting worse, and she was already legally blind. The doctor's report was that she would be totally blind in a short time with nothing they could do to help her.

I put my arm around her and began to pray for her and immediately received a word of knowledge from the Holy Spirit. I boldly spoke it out and said, "What happened to you when you were eight years old to bring rejection into your life?"

She started to cry and said the rejection came from her father. "You must forgive him, regardless of what brought about the rejection," I told her. I carefully led her in a prayer, as she forgave him and asked God to forgive her for holding resentment for him all those years. She felt a great relief and went on her way.

About a year passed and this lady came up to me and said, "You don't remember me do you?" I looked at her and she did look vaguely familiar, but I had to admit I did not remember her. Then she told me her story. She had been living in Panama City and was very despondent, when a friend asked her to attend the conference. This friend had paid her way and arranged transportation for her since her eyes were too bad to drive. After attending my workshop, she went forward for prayer, and that's when I gave her the word of knowledge. Now she was able to tell me about the rejection that had occurred when she was eight.

Her mother and father had divorced when she was a little girl, and she lived with her father. After a couple of years her father remarried and in due time her stepmother went to the hospital to give birth to a baby girl. Her father had gone to the hospital to bring her stepmother and the baby home. They lived in an apartment building and when the elevator came up to her floor, she was waiting right there in the hallway. Then her father stepped out of the elevator holding a newborn baby girl in his arms and proudly proclaimed, "Ann, this is your replacement." She was only eight years old and did not understand that he meant the new baby was her replacement as the baby of the family. She thought that this was his new daughter and she would no longer hold that position.

From that day forward, she had felt rejection, even though she did not understand it. There was a sadness in her life that she had never been able to get the victory over, and she did not know the origin of it. Because she did not understand forgiveness or even that she needed to forgive him, she had been held in bondage all those years. He had placed her in bondage with five words without even realizing it.

The day I prayed with her and led her to forgive her dad, things started to happen in her life. Her eyes seemed to improve, whereas the doctor had said they would only get worse. So she went back to the doctor to see what the situation was. He seemed surprised and said there seemed to be a remission in the inherited disorder, and she was a candidate for eye surgery that should correct the sight problems. This had not been an option before, but now he was convinced it would work. The surgery was completed and sure enough, her sight was restored. When forgiveness came, healing also came.

At the time this story began, some three years ago, Ann lived in Panama City, Florida, with a very bleak future. She could do very little due to her failing eyesight. Here was a very talented lady with so much to give to God's people but with a handicap she did not know how to overcome. Due to forgiveness, she now drives her own car, works full-time at *Charisma* magazine in Lake

Mary, Florida, with her talents shining as she furthers the kingdom of God.

ARTHRITIS

Many times we are seeking healing and it just doesn't seem to come to pass. Then we cannot understand why. James 5:16 sheds some light on the problem: "Confess your trespasses to one another, and pray for one another, that you may be healed." When you confess that you have trespassed against a brother, that is the same as asking forgiveness, because you recognize that you have trespassed against him. I have found that most times when people who have arthritis problems are not healed, it is because they have trespassed against someone and not confessed it, or someone has trespassed against them.

One such instance happened to me some years back when I was at church on Wednesday night. This little older lady was sitting immediately on my left. We sang a couple of songs, and then the pastor suggested we pray for the person sitting beside us. I turned to this lady and asked her what her need was. I immediately noticed her hands were gnarled and crooked because of arthritis. "I would like to be happy like you are," was her immediate response.

"Are you saved and on your way to heaven?" I asked.

"Evidently I'm not," she answered, "for you definitely have something I don't."

I led her in a sinner's prayer so she would be born again. Then I asked her about her hands and the crippling arthritis that was attacking them. She informed me they had been that way for some years but had been getting worse lately.

"Is there someone you need to forgive? Someone who hurt you and you still feel resentment toward them?" I gently prodded her.

She thought a moment and then replied that her mother had always put her down. She had gotten married at a young age to get away from her, and her mother had berated her for that as well as many other things. She had raised one daughter, but her life had never been very happy. She resented the fact that she had not been happy. She had been involved with Christian Science but had been unable to get help there. Her husband was sickly, and there seemed to be more trouble than she could handle.

"You need to forgive your mom and let the blood of Jesus cover that," I interrupted her. "I'm sure she had no intention of making you miserable. Circumstances came about that brought the unhappiness in your life." She nodded agreement, and I led her in that simple forgiveness prayer and at the end prayed for her hands to be healed and straightened. By this time the service was continuing, and we did not get an opportunity to talk any further.

Two days later the phone in the office rang. It was the lady, and she said the arthritis was totally gone. Before we prayed, she had large lumps on the palms of her hands that were very painful, and holes between the lumps were so deep that she had to use a cotton swab to cleanse the indentures. She wanted me to know that her hands were now perfectly normal, and the doctor had decreased her insulin intake.

This lady's daughter called and offered to help stuff the newsletter. I always had a time of prayer after the work was completed, so when we were done, I invited her on down to the office and prayed for her. She, too, received a deep healing in her body. I then accompanied her to her house and led her dad to the Lord. It was the last days of his life, but he received salvation before passing on. Her mom lived a good Christian life for some years before joining her husband in death. All this came about because of a simple little forgiveness prayer. Oh yes, another thing—at church, the Sunday following her healing, her daughter received Jesus as her Savior.

BACK PROBLEMS

A certain principle comes about quite often with back problems. One such incident happened recently when I was ministering on Sunday morning in a church not far from our home. One mature gentleman, who was of African descent, came forward with severe back problems. "How long have you been bothered with this problem?" I asked him.

"Since World War II," he quietly answered. "For over fifty years I have suffered because of wounds I received in the Philippines."

"It's time to get rid of it," I told him. "First, I want you to forgive the enemy who shot you, and then forgive the U. S. Army that sent you over there, as well as the prejudice that prevailed in the armed services at that time."

He quickly agreed and I led him, as he, with his own voice, forgave each one. Then I prayed a prayer of healing. He was slain in the spirit and came up a little later a new man. That night he was back in church services and proclaimed it was the first time in over fifty years he had been without any pain whatsoever. Praise God!

CHAPTER 15

Forgiveness Brings Unity

Jesus taught us that we must have unity above all else.

There is one body and one Spirit, just as you were called in one hope of your calling; one Lord, one faith, one baptism; one God and Father of all, who is above all, and through all, and in you all. But to each one of us grace was given according to the measure of Christ's gift. . . . And He Himself gave some to be apostles, some prophets, some evangelists, and some pastors and teachers, for the equipping of the saints for the work of ministry, for the edifying of the body of Christ, till we all come to the unity of the faith and of the knowledge of the Son of God, to a perfect man, to the measure of the stature of the fullness of Christ . . ."

—EPHESIANS 4:4–7, 11–13

The Bible teaches: "Therefore, as the elect of God, holy and beloved, put on tender mercies, kindness, humility, meekness, longsuffering: bearing with one another, and forgiving one another, if anyone has a complaint against another; even as Christ forgave you, so you also must do" (Col. 3:12–13).

This leaves us no choice in the matter, only a decision. If we plan to follow God, we must forgive.

Jesus said, "Take heed to yourselves. If thy brother sins against you, rebuke him; and if he repents, forgive him. And if he sins against you seven times in a day, and seven times in a day returns to you, saying, 'I repent,' you shall forgive him" (Luke 17:3–4). Wow! This looks as if we must forgive. If we plan to be holy and beloved of God, then we must forgive.

MENDING A BROKEN RELATIONSHIP

Many times when we are faced with the need to forgive it is a difficult decision to make. Some years ago I was the administrative assistant to an evangelist and operated the ministry when he was out of town traveling and doing the work of the Lord. A brother minister came in and was extremely mad at the evangelist, who was not there that day. He took all his anger out on me. He demanded that I give him a check for a stated amount, and he wanted it right then. Eventually he stopped yelling and calmed down somewhat. At that point I tried, very politely, to tell him I did not have the authority to do what he asked. That authority had to come from the ministry board.

Again, he raised his voice, and I, being a female, thought about crying but instead decided to stand my ground and use my "office authority." When I realized there was no appeasing him, I asked him to please leave

157

the office. He eventually complied, but our relationship from that time on was very cool. We still had frequent contact and a lot of close mutual friends. This became increasingly difficult, even though I asked him to forgive me for not being able to do as he demanded. (I felt his demands were totally unreasonable.) He was always rigid and quite curt with me.

I found a scripture in Colossians 1:19–20: "For it pleased the Father that in Him all the fullness should dwell, by Him to reconcile all things to Himself, by Him, whether things on earth or things in heaven, having made peace through the blood of His cross." This told me that the blood of Jesus would reconcile all things, and I began to pray this scripture over this minister. (He had withdrawn from the ministry I worked for about three months prior and started a new work of his own in the same town.) Only three weeks after I prayed this prayer daily and forgave him, he called and asked my husband and me to minister at a Sweetheart Banquet and speak on forgiveness. This, in turn, brought about a complete healing in our relationship. God is awesome!

UNITY IN MARRIAGE

Jesus taught regarding prayer: "I say to you that if two of you agree on earth concerning anything that they ask, it will be done for them by My Father in heaven" (Matt. 18:19). Jesus wants us to walk in forgiveness and unity in every area of our lives. We are told in 1 Peter 3:7 for husbands and wives to be in unity "so that your prayers may not be hindered." When these two scriptures are combined, we find that one of the strongest prayers in the world is for the husband and wife to be in unity and to ask the Father for the desires of their hearts.

I am reminded of a couple in another state that we

ministered to some years back. She was really sold out to the Lord, and she and her three daughters were in church almost every time the church door opened. Her husband professed to be a Christian, but it was difficult to believe him because he never wanted to go to church. It was quite a bone of contention between them.

The wife decided to invite my husband and me to their house for dinner and see if they could get some issues settled between them.

The night we were to be there, their smallest little girl, about eight years old, called and asked if we could be there thirty minutes early so she could show my husband something in the yard before darkness fell. We agreed and arrived at the appointed time. Sherrie, the little girl, took my husband by the hand and led him around the house to where she had planted a shrubbery specimen. My husband was knowledgeable about shrubbery in this local area, so she wanted him to see it and see what his comments would be. They talked about it for quite some time as her dad, James, looked on. James was impressed for he really loved and understood his daughter. He thought, *If this man would take the time and effort to talk with my little girl, then I can listen to what he and his wife have to say about my marriage.*

We had a great meal together, with the three girls doing a lot of the talking. Afterward, the mom put the kids in their rooms, and the four of us sat down in the living room and began to discuss their problems.

"James doesn't want to go to church most of the time, and the girls and I feel like he doesn't love us," Doris stated, wasting no time in getting things out in the open. James just looked at her and didn't say anything.

My husband waited a few minutes and then asked, "What kind of work do you do, James?"

"I'm a brick mason," he answered the question but

went no further with the conversation.

"A brick mason is an extremely physical job," I commented, choosing my words carefully. "What time do you go to work in the morning?"

"I'm usually on the job at 7:00 A.M. To be there and ready to work by no later than 7:00, I am up and going by 5:30 each morning." All this was matter-of-factly stated, with no emphasis placed on any portion.

"Then what time do you get home in the afternoon?" my husband asked, getting back into the conversation at this point.

"Usually by about 5 o'clock. A lot depends on just where I am working that day. If we are building on a brick house or neighborhood on the other side of town, it takes longer to drive and sometimes I may be up by 5 in the morning and not back home until 6 that night."

"What about you, Doris?" I inquired. "Do you get up at the same time James does? Do you work on a public job? What is your schedule?"

"I don't get up at the same time James does, because he doesn't mind preparing his own breakfast. The girls and I get up usually around 6:30, and they get ready to go to school. It would be so much nicer if they could see their dad in the morning, but he is always gone to work by the time they get up . . ." Her voice drifted off as she completed the last sentence. As we talked a little further we discovered that she didn't work outside the home and did most of the home repair and yard work. I could sense there was resentment because of this.

"In other words, you don't see your girls, except when you come home in the late afternoon during the week?" I queried, shifting my attention back to James, and he nodded his head in agreement. "Do you miss not getting to see them?" I asked. Again, he nodded.

I could see a pattern in their lives that was creating the

problems. When James came in from work on Wednesday, tired and dirty, Doris and the girls were dressed and ready to go to Wednesday night church service. He resented the whole situation and that they seemed to have no time for him. He knew that he should go to church, but the circumstances of their lifestyle had so discouraged him that he didn't even want to go to church on Sunday, the one day he did have the time.

As we talked it out with the two of them, they each began to see what their problem was. Doris had not understood that James was constrained by time and circumstances on Wednesday and, for that matter, any other night church service. Her day had been spent at home, so she could arrange her schedule around the service and work with the girls to get them ready to go. As we pointed this out, she understood.

At the same time, James had not understood that Doris resented him not doing some of the home repair and yard work. He had felt like she was home during the day and could arrange her day to suit her and the girls. They both came to a fresh understanding of the other's work and the problems their general lifestyle had placed on their relationship.

We led each of them in a forgiveness prayer as they both truly repented for areas in which they had held each other in bondage. What a change came in their lives from that day forward. Doris did not expect James to go to church in the middle of the week, and this released him from bondage and condemnation. As a result, he was again happy to be in church when his schedule permitted. Because of the released resentment in both their lives, they began to pray together and God blessed their family. Their girls now had two parents, both of whom they truly loved, and it was obvious to everyone who saw the family together. God will truly bless your family if you will just give Him the chance!

But do solutions like this last? God does all things well, and He brings about solutions that continue through the years. This family is still intact to this day and doing well.

Expectations

_vs_

Forgiveness

Part 4

....

Blessings, Freedom and Fire

....

CHAPTER 16

Release and Bless Through the Name of Jesus

God has taught us repeatedly that whatever we sow, we will reap. Therefore, if we bless, then we will inherit His blessing. There is nothing greater in this life than to have the blessings of God upon us each day of our lives. This becomes so plain as we read 1 Peter 3:8–9: "Finally, all of you be of one mind, having compassion for one another; love as brothers, be tenderhearted, be courteous; not returning evil for evil or reviling for reviling, but on the contrary blessing, knowing that you were called to this, that you may inherit a blessing."

In the Sermon on the Mount, Jesus taught the multitudes: "You have heard that it was said, 'You shall love your neighbor and hate your enemy.' But I say to you, love your enemies, bless those who curse you, do good to those who hate you, and pray for those who spitefully use you and persecute you" (Matt. 5:43–44). Not only did Jesus tell us to release, but He also told us to bless. It is of utmost importance to release everyone from unforgiveness (which in turn releases us), but it is equally important to then bless them.

When I teach this, many people say, "But how can I bless someone who has caused me so much harm?" That's a hard question, but Jesus has the answer. They did Him "so wrong," and even hung Him on the cross and still He forgave them and blessed them. In our flesh, it seems impossible to bless someone who has spitefully used us, and yet Jesus said to do just that. The answer is that we must do it "in the name of Jesus." That was the reason He died on the cross to start with — to take our sins, to take our iniquities, to take our trespasses, to take our sorrow, to take our poverty, to take our unhappiness. He showed us the way, but it is up to each of us to appropriate the exchange He made at the cross and receive His blessings.

BLESSING OUR LOVED ONES

It is of utmost importance to bless those who despitefully use you, but just as important is that you bless your loved ones. We read in the Old Testament where the Jewish patriarchs always called their offspring together before their death and prayed a father's blessing over each of them. We have found that few Christians today have ever had a father's blessing prayed over them. In fact, many have even been estranged from their fathers and walk in unforgiveness. As my husband and I minister, it has been our custom, after we have ministered on forgiveness and prayed with people to be released and led them in a prayer, then my husband prays a father's blessing over them. There are numerous ways to pray a blessing, but I will give you an example of one he often prays that is based on Genesis 49:25 and following. This is only the starting point and he uses his own words after that.

> "By the God of your father who will help you, and
>   by the Almighty who will bless you
> With blessings of heaven above, blessings of the
>   deep that lies beneath,
> I proclaim: Blessings of prosperity as you are obe-
>   dient in your tithes . . .
> Blessings of health in your physical body . . .
> Blessings of long life as you continue to serve the
>   Lord thy God . . .
> Blessings of peace and happiness for you and your
>   entire family . . .
> You will be blessed as you come in and as you go
>   out...
> And all that your hand touches will prosper.
> I proclaim this father's blessing on you this day . . .
> In the name of the Father and the Son and the Holy
>   Ghost . . . Amen."

As you can see by this blessing, spoken words become a blessing in a person's life. Words can affect us in three different ways. First, in Matthew 12:36 Jesus said, "Every idle word that men shall speak, they shall give account of . . ." An idle word is a non-effective word. Second, if there are idle, or non-effective words, then conversely speaking, there are effective words, as well. Third, there are word curses. So then, the three types of words we speak are: (1) an effective word (2) an idle word (3) a word curse. God's people are constantly speaking curses on other people, completely unintention-ally, and causing many problems. Every time we speak, I personally believe that we should strive for an effective word, or, might I say, a faith-filled word.

Many years ago, when our daughter Karen was a little

girl, perhaps ten years old, we had a yearly problem. Each summer she would get a bee sting just before we went on vacation so she couldn't wear her shoes due to the swelling. Each summer we would say: "Next week is vacation, and she will get a bee sting and not be able to wear her shoes." Sure enough, that would be exactly what would happen. Finally, our little aunt in North Carolina said, "You're putting a curse on her with your mouth." My husband and I looked at each other in amazement but knew that what she was saying was the truth. We knew we should have been blessing but just were neglectful about doing it.

From that point on, my husband and I changed what we were saying. We blessed her with our words and spoke encouragement to her. Our words dispersed ministering angels to look out for her, and she never had another bee sting. Prior to us speaking blessings over her, she had broken her arm two or three times. After we changed our speech, never again did she have a broken bone. We discovered that watching our words not only changed her life, but it also changed our lives as well. We have spent our years striving to bless our offspring. My husband still prays daily for prosperity for our children and for wisdom to handle the prosperity.

We read in James 3:8–11: "But no man can tame the tongue. It is an unruly evil, full of deadly poison. With it we bless our God and Father, and with it we curse men, who have been made in the similitude of God. Out of the same mouth proceed blessing and cursing. My brethren, these things ought not to be so. Does a spring send forth fresh water and bitter from the same opening?" Think on this scripture and see if it doesn't change your life.

Medical Diagnoses

Another area of unintentional cursing that is so prevalent in today's society is a medical diagnostic curse. The doctor examines you and speaks the worst possible diagnosis. Why? In many instances doctors have been sued because they did not bring back a serious diagnosis, and when the person later died, the family was furious. The definition of *diagnosis* is "the recognizing or naming of a disease by studying its symptoms." Doctors have discovered that if they give a bad diagnosis first and the problem proves to be less serious, their patients never complain about that. So, they are speak out the worst possible scenario, just to protect themselves from being sued. In reality, that is a word curse.

Anytime a doctor speaks out a negative diagnosis, we should break the word curse that has been spoken over us or our loved ones. In turn we should speak blessings over the person. "But isn't that denying the facts?" you may ask. Not at all. Even if it is an accurate diagnosis, it is still a curse and should be broken and a blessing spoken instead. Facts change daily, but God is the same yesterday, today, and forever. We, as God's people, must learn to talk correctly, and bless instead of curse.

What the doctor said may be a true fact. But God's Word, which says "by His stripes you are healed," is a truth that supersedes the natural realm of fact. "Now faith is the substance of things hoped for and the evidence of things not seen" (Heb. 11:1). You and the doctor see yourself as sick, but God sees you healed. Which is the greater power—the disease or God?

When I first got saved and began to try to obey God's commandments, I had trouble with this very principle. If I got the sniffles and started sneezing, I would also run into several people who would say, "I see you're catching a cold." I had such a hard time trying to figure out what to say that would not make me sound super-spiritual but also would not make negative confessions. I asked the Lord to give me words to say, and He told me that it was OK to rehearse my positive confession. So the next time I sneezed and got the usual, "Are you catching a cold?" I answered with, "Just getting over it." That was the truth, and yet it was the positive truth, not negative. Even though I might have had the germs for only a matter of minutes, I had already started the battle to get free from the malady. I could speak the truth, not sound super-spiritual, and still be positive. Praise God!

If I do have to go to the doctor and get medicine, then my prayer is that the medicine will help to heal my physical body and have no adverse effects on me. If people ask me, "How are you doing?" I simply answer them: "I'm taking my medicine, praying over it and getting better every day." That's the truth, and yet it's the positive truth.

LOVING OUR ENEMIES

The Bible says in 1 John 3:13: "Do not marvel, my brethren, if the world hates you." In Matthew 5:44, Jesus said, "Do good to those who hate you." If we combine these two scriptures we find that we are to do good to the people who are not Christians, and thereby, through the power of God as we pray for them, they may become saved in due time. What a concept God has for us to live by. First, we are to "get free," and then, through obeying His Word, we can help others "get free."

Continuing on in 1 John 3:15–16: "Whoever hates his brother is a murderer, and you know that no murderer has eternal life abiding in him. By this we know love, because He laid down His life for us. And we also ought to lay down our lives for the brethren."

We usually mope around and complain if we even have to be civil to those who hate us. Jesus said that if we have a chance to do good to those who hate us, we would be blessed. "But I say to you, love your enemies, bless those who curse you, do good to those who hate you, and pray for those who spitefully use you and persecute you" (Matt. 5:44).

One other thing Jesus said in Matthew 5:44 was to pray for those who persecute you. The thinking of the world is exactly the opposite, "Whatever they do to you, do it back to them, with interest." If we are to get free, then we have to renew our minds and think like God thinks. He almost always thinks exactly opposite to the thinking of the world. In this instance Jesus says to pray for our persecutors. Why should we pray for someone who persecutes us? The answer is so simple. If we pray for them, then they can be set free, which in turn will change the world, and greatly increase God's kingdom, and bring His will to pass.

CHAPTER 17

Walk in Freedom as You Change Your Mind

When we receive Jesus and are saved, we change where we will spend eternity. To change our present life here on earth, we need to change our minds from worldly thinking to godly thinking. To do this we need to be transformed by the renewing of our minds. This is what the Word tells us to do.

> And do not be conformed to this world, but be transformed by the renewing of your mind, that you may prove what is that good and acceptable and perfect will of God.
>
> —ROMANS 12:2

The word *transformed* is translated from the Greek word *metamorphoo*. This is the same as our English word *metamorphosis*, which means "to change, transfigure, or transform." In fact, there are two examples that readily come to mind that we can witness with our eyes. One is the tadpole, who, through the process of metamorphosis, turns into a frog. The next one is even more exciting, for in this example an unsightly caterpillar makes a cocoon and after a period of time emerges as a beautiful butterfly. What a transformation! That's what God wants us to do. He wants us to make a cocoon with the Word of God, and, after time passes, we emerge as a mature Christians, walking in victory, and furthering the kingdom of God here on earth.

CREATING NEW THOUGHTS

Your mind must be renewed by the Word of God. If only you can grasp onto this principle, then your life will be changed.

Ephesians 4:23 says, "And be renewed in the *spirit* of your mind." The NIV translates this as: "the *attitude* of your mind. In order for your mind to change, your attitude must change. A positive attitude will bring about a positive result, and a negative attitude will bring about a negative result. Always believe it is possible to solve your problems, for tremendous things happen to the believer.

Here are the steps to take in renewing your mind and attitude:

1. **Conditioned thoughts.** These are thoughts that you put into your mind on purpose. You program them in by intentionally thinking these thoughts. These conditioned thoughts will in turn lead you to . . .
2. **Repeated thoughts.** These are the thoughts that go through your mind again and again. If you have repeated thoughts, they will lead you to . . .
3 **Thought habits.** Anything that is repeated over

and over again soon becomes habit forming. We can certainly pick up bad habits quickly. It takes a little bit longer to acquire good habits, but they are habits, just the same. Thought habits lead to . . .

4. **Attitude.** Your habits directly influence your attitude. If you think negatively, then your attitude will be negative; and if you are a positive thinker, then your attitude will be positive. Your attitude will in turn dictate your . . .

5. **Actions**, which are your outward behavior.

This whole process is what the Bible calls "renewing your mind." To start the process, you must make the Word of God your source for *conditioned thoughts*. This means that you search the Bible to find good thoughts to think. For instance, think on Philippians 4:7: "And the peace of God, which surpasses all understanding, will guard your hearts and minds through Christ Jesus."

That is a good thought to condition into your thought patterns. Another excellent thought is in verse 13: "I can do all things through Christ who strengthens me." If you will condition that thought into your mind, repeat it often, that one verse will change your life.

Further on in verse 19, we find a powerful promise: "And my God shall supply all your need according to His riches in glory by Christ Jesus."

Isn't it amazing how many good thoughts there are in just one chapter of the Bible! Can you see the importance of conditioned thoughts?

Norman Vincent Peale in his book, *The Power of Positive Thinking,* said, "Formulate and stamp indelibly on your mind a mental picture of yourself as succeeding." There is some truth to this statement, if it is brought in line with God and His power.

LEARNING HOW TO CONFESS

We are a product of what we say. This is true even in the business realm. If you have ever been involved in sales of any type you will understand what I mean. You are taught to set a goal and then tell other salespeople in your district that you are going to sell a certain amount of goods during that period. As you say it with your mouth, a certain amount of truth will enter into the situation simply through the power of saying it with your mouth.

The reason is that we are created in God's image (Gen. 1:27), and God has what He says! When He said, "Let there be light," there was light. Since we are created in God's own image, we have the authority to open our mouths and put in motion what we desire for the future.

Sometimes people tell me, "Confession just does not work for me. I do not have what I say," or, "I cannot say it if I do not have it. These things of confession do not work." There is only one answer for this: JESUS SAID IT WOULD!

> Now in the morning, as they passed by, they saw the fig tree dried up from the roots. And Peter, remembering, said to Him, "Rabbi, look! The fig tree which You cursed has withered away." So Jesus answered and said to them, "Have faith in God. For assuredly, I say to you, whoever says to this mountain, 'Be removed and be cast into the sea,' and does not doubt in his heart, but believes that those things he says will be done, he will have whatever he says. Therefore I say to you, whatever things you ask when you pray, believe that you receive them and you will have them."
>
> —MARK 11:20–24

If it isn't working, let's see if we can find out why. If we can get it working, then we can plan our future with the words of our mouths and the faith in our hearts. I suggest that the first thing you do is to make a confession about how you feel about the Word of God. I would even suggest that you write it in the front of your Bible. *"This is the Word of God! I can do what it says I can do! This is God speaking to me! What it says I have, belongs to me! I am what it says I am!"*

Is this your confession? If it is not your confession, pray and ask God if it should be. If you want the Word to really work in your life, either this or a similar confession must be yours.

If only we could realize that God's Word is God speaking to us! When it says in 1 Peter 2:24, "By His stripes we were healed," that is God speaking directly to us. Then we can say, "That belongs to me, and I will fight for it."

If the doctor has diagnosed you with diabetes, cancer, TMJ (pain in joints and muscles of the jaw), carpal tunnel syndrome, or other physical problems, you have the authority through the name of Jesus and His blood to speak to the root cause and apply the Word of God.

In the natural realm a tree surgeon would apply Root Kill to a stump after a tree has been cut down to destroy the root system of the diagnosed disease. If you don't kill the root of the tree, then it will begin to sprout and grow again. In the spiritual realm you can use God's Word like Root Kill.

Matthew 15:13 says, "Every plant which My heavenly Father has not planted shall be rooted up." Ask yourself, "Did God plant this disease in me?" He can't be your healer and your destroyer. He gave you power and authority over all the words of the devil. Sickness and disease is planted in you by the destroyer, Satan. Health and well-being are given to you by Jesus. Let your mouth be the root killer of the disease by applying the Word of God as a root killer.

In the story of the fig tree, the literal Greek meaning says, "Have faith in God." Every believer has a measure of faith, and the Bible says that Jesus is the author and finisher of our faith. (See Hebrews 12:2.) I believe He authors things that are good, and He finishes them completely. So God did not author a halfway faith in us. He gives us the God kind of faith.

Jesus described what the God-kind of faith could do: "For assuredly, I say to you, whoever says to this mountain, 'Be removed and be cast into the sea,' and does not doubt in his heart, but believes that those things he says will be done, he will have whatever he says. Therefore I say to you, whatever things you ask when you pray, believe that you receive them, and you will have them" (Mark 11:23–24).

Jesus said that the man who has faith "shall have whatever he says." Without changing the meaning of that verse we can say: *I can have whatsoever I say.* That will make it personal to us.

Now, let's think about the condition that Jesus said is necessary "[Whoever] shall not doubt in his heart, but believes that those things he says will be done, he will have whatever he says." What Jesus is actually saying is that you can have everything that comes forth from your mouth if you meets the conditions.

If you study the ministry of Christ you will never find a place where He uses the words *maybe, if, but,* or any other negative word of unbelief. When people came up to Him and said, "You can heal me if You will," He always said, "I will."

He always went about things positively. When he prayed, He said, "Father, I know that You hear me, and I pray that these here might believe." I have examined how many great men and women of faith prayed for healing for those in the prayer lines. The words of their prayers were often for the benefit of the people in the line, for their faith was reaching to God already. The only thing necessary to say is, "Be healed," and the Word comes to pass.

We have every right as believers to walk up to a sick body and say, "I command you to correct yourself. Get in line with the Word of God, in the name of Jesus." We can have what we say if we have no doubt in our hearts.

GETTING RID OF DOUBT

What is our heart? The heart is the center of our being. The heart of an apple is the very center of it. When we get to the heart of a problem, we get to the root of the problem. If the heart is the center of our being, then our heart must be our spirit.

Doubt is anything that is contrary to God's Word. In Numbers 13, we read of the twelve spies for the children of Israel who went to scout out the Promised Land. Two of them said, "We are well able to take the land." They saw the giants in the land but they reported *faith*. The Bible says the other ten gave an "evil" report, for they said, "We be not able." Evidently, anything contrary to God is an evil report.

God had already told them the land belonged to them. All they had to do was go in and possess it. Instead of confessing God's plan, the ten complained, "We are as grasshoppers in their sight." The Bible says that was an evil report, for it was a report of doubt and unbelief, contrary to what God had told them.

People today are going about saying, "I just cannot do that. I cannot receive this." What we need to do is line up

179

what we believe in our hearts, say it with our mouths, and it will come to pass. We can have whatever we say if we believe it in our hearts.

How do we believe in our heart? First, we must realize what God's Word is. We must realize that it is the final authority for every situation. We see what God's Word says about every situation, and then we line up our speech with the Word of God.

CONFESSION SAFEGUARDS

Empty confessions of the mouth are not worth anything. Much confusion has come into the body of Christ because of this. People have said: "I confess a new car. I confess a new home. I confess this and that." It is not that simple. First your confession must agree with the Word.

God knew what He was doing when He wrote the Bible. It was not written by someone who did not know how the laws of the Spirit operate. He put safeguards in it. There are certain things for which we cannot believe. For example, we cannot believe for things that will be contrary to our health or someone else's health, or contrary to the Word of God. It cannot be done. We cannot believe and operate in faith concerning those things.

But for the good things in life, we can operate in faith. The Word of God says all good and perfect gifts come from God. (See James 1:17.) You can believe for any good thing that you desire. If you can believe for it in the heart and say it with the mouth you can have it.

Romans 10:9–10 says: "If you confess with your mouth the Lord Jesus and believe in your heart that God has raised Him from the dead, you will be saved. For with the heart one believes unto righteousness, and with the mouth confession is made unto salvation."

Believing and confessing are our part, and grace is

God's part. "By grace you have been saved" (Eph. 2:5). Grace has been defined as "God's unconditional positive regard," but these words are only a man's definition. God's grace is beyond definition as far as man is concerned.

The Bible tells us that we need the words of our mouths to be saved. Confess Jesus as Lord and you shall be saved. If you ask a non-believer if he believes Jesus died and God raised Him from the dead, sometimes he might say, "Sure, I believe that." That person is still not saved. He can believe that all he wants to, but he is still not born again.

Next, you must explain to the non-believer, "If you believe that, then I want you to confess Jesus as your Lord." If the man says, "Jesus is my Lord," at that moment a great miracle takes place. That man is born again in that very instant. He becomes a new creation in Christ Why? Not because he believes, though that is a necessary part of it. The thing that transformed him was when he said with his mouth, "Jesus is my Lord!" God puts a premium on the words of our mouths!

TALK RIGHT

With all this in mind, think how important it is for us to talk right. Believers in the past have said, "That tickles me to death!" or "I laughed so much that I thought I was going to die laughing." In contrast, the Bible says, "A merry heart does good, like medicine" (Prov. 11:22). To be scripturally correct, we should say, "I laughed so much I thought I would live forever." I ask you now, is that not a better way to say it?

If we died the first time we said, "That tickles me to death," or "That scared me to death," the world would really be in a mess. Sometimes we get disgusted with someone and say, "Oh, he makes me sick." The Word of

God says the words of our mouths are health to our flesh. (See Proverbs 4:20–22.) This indicates that positive words actually give healing to the body, so negative words must do the opposite. Don't make yourself sick with your own words!

We need to get in line with God's Word. When the Lord told Joshua how to be prosperous in everything he did, He said, "Let not these words depart out of your mouth" (Josh. 1:8). How do you not let them depart out of your mouth? Keep talking them! This does not mean you have to say all the *thee*'s and *thou*'s. It means talk positive, talk faith, talk power, talk success. Do not talk doubt and unbelief. It will defeat you.

If you talk doubt and unbelief and it defeats you, what will happen if you talk in agreement with God's Word? It will exalt you, that's what! It will exalt you in every part of your body.

Jesus warned the Pharisees: "Brood of vipers! How can you, being evil, speak good things? For out of the abundance of the heart the mouth speaks. A good man out of the good treasure of his heart brings forth good things, and an evil man out of the evil treasure brings forth evil things. But I say to you that for every idle word men may speak, they will give account of it in the day of judgment. For by your words you will be justified, and by your words you will be condemned" (Matt. 12:34–37).

If we are born again, we should have such an abundance of the Word of God in our hearts that it spills out when we speak.

God's Word says you are justified by the very words of your mouth. It says that every idle word that men shall speak, they shall give account for. Do you know what "idle word" means? I believe it means an ineffective word. How many people do you know who talk a lot and never really say anything? If we don't have something to say, why don't we just keep quiet?

The Bible says we will be held accountable for every ineffective word that we speak. If we are going to be held accountable for something that is ineffective, then we should not say it. The total of all this adds up to the fact that we should always say only positive words, and never negative words. If you can make this decision, here and now, it will literally change your life.

Help me God to say only positive words!

....

CHAPTER 18

Jesus Baptizes With the Holy Ghost and Fire

I have often been asked, "Why do I need the baptism in the Holy Spirit?" Let's look at things logically and see whether the baptism of the Holy Spirit is really for you. Also why do some people not receive the baptism? Let's find out, by searching the Bible, just what we should do to receive the baptism.

After Jesus had been crucified and risen from the dead, He joined two disciples who were walking on the road to Emmaus (Luke 24). The two disciples were talking, and Jesus asked them about their conversation. They told him they were talking about Jesus of Nazareth, who was a prophet mighty in deed and word. Then they said some of their group had gone to the tomb early and found it empty and saw only a vision of angels who said Jesus was alive.

Then Jesus said to them, "O foolish ones, and slow of heart to believe in all that the prophets have spoken!

Ought not the Christ to have suffered these things and to enter into His glory?" (Luke 24:25–26).

What did the prophets speak? They prophesied many details about Jesus' birth, life, death, and resurrection. Isaiah 11:1–2 described Jesus: "There shall come forth a Rod from the stem of Jesse, And a Branch shall grow out of his roots, The Spirit of the Lord shall rest upon Him, The Spirit of wisdom and understanding, The Spirit of knowledge and of the fear of the Lord." Isaiah 53 gave many details about His death. The disciples knew all that the prophets said, and they had seen Jesus' miracles, yet they were still slow about believing. No wonder we are slow today. Nothing has changed. That's why we need the Holy Spirit's help.

In Joel 2:28–29 we read: "And it shall come to pass afterward that I will pour out My Spirit on all flesh; Your sons and your daughters shall prophesy, your old men shall dream dreams, Your young men shall see visions, and also on My menservants and on My maidservants I will pour out My Spirit in those days." This is a promise to you and to me.

Have you ever tried reading the Bible, and it actually made very little sense to you? If you have, then you definitely need the power and the boldness of the Holy Spirit to come into you to open the Scriptures to you.

Neither you, nor the seminary, nor the theologians, nor the people who teach at the big schools are going to teach you the Bible. It is the Holy Spirit, who is going to do it. Let's read on as Jesus expounded the Scriptures for the two disciples on the road to Emmaus: "Now it came to pass, as He sat at the table with them, that He took bread, blessed and broke it, and gave it to them. Then their eyes were opened and they knew Him; and He vanished from their sight. And they said to one another, 'Did not our heart burn within us while He talked with us on the road, and while He opened the Scriptures to us?'" (Luke 24:30).

When you receive the Holy Spirit, He is the one who is going to teach you the Bible. It is God, the Holy Spirit, who is going to reveal it to you. So, why do you need the baptism of the Holy Spirit? That is a good enough reason right there. If you are going to follow in God's Word, you have to understand it. The Holy Spirit is the one who will do that!

When my husband and I were first baptized in the Holy Spirit, we had an intense hunger to read the Bible like we had never had before. We literally devoured the Word for months. Even until today, we each, on our own, read through the Bible every year. Each year we find new revelations as God opens the Scriptures to us.

Why do I need the baptism in the Holy Spirit? Jesus said in John 14:15–17, "If you love Me, keep My commandments. And I will pray the Father, and He will give you another Helper, that He may abide with you forever — the Spirit of Truth, whom the world cannot receive, because it neither sees Him nor knows Him; but you know Him, for He dwells with you and will be in you."

Jesus said the Holy Spirit shall be "in you." Then He continued: "I will not leave you orphans; I will come to you" (v. 18). We know that Jesus rose from the dead and ascended to the right hand of the Father. But He said, "I will come to you." I think He meant that He would come by way of the Spirit. Jesus really made it plain when He said: "But the Helper, the Holy Spirit, whom the father will send in My name, He will teach you all things, and bring to your remembrance all things that I said to you" (John 14:26).

This is how the Holy Spirit is going to come inside you and teach you the Bible, which is the words of Jesus.

PRODUCE FRUIT

Why else do you need the Holy Spirit? You need to produce fruit. Fruit comes from the power and the boldness of the Holy Spirit. Jesus said in John 15:1–2: "I am the true vine, and My Father is the vine-dresser. Every branch in Me that does not bear fruit He takes away; and every branch that bears fruit He prunes, that it may bear more fruit."

Stop and think about that. You received the Lord in your heart and perhaps have even received the baptism of the Holy Spirit. Is fruit evident in your life? Are you witnessing to people? Do you have the boldness that you need? Did He give you the anointing so that you can go and produce fruit? This is what you are here for!

He has some work left for each and every one of us to do. God wants someone who has a yielded heart. He needs someone to say, "Yes, Lord! I have already signed the check, You fill it out!"

We can say, "Yes, Lord!" but stepping out and *doing* the work is another matter. He made each of us with a free will. If we have a free will, then we need to decide exactly what we will do. He always wants us to choose Him, but He will not impose Himself on us.

Jesus continued teaching: "You are already clean because of the word which I have spoken to you. Abide in me, and I in you. As the branch cannot bear fruit of itself, unless it abides in the vine, neither can you, unless you abide in Me. I am the vine, you are the branches. He who abides in Me, and I in him, bears much fruit, for without Me you can do nothing" (John 15:3–5). Remember that, for without Him we cannot do anything!

Jesus continued teaching and in John 15:26 and again made it very plain, "But when the Helper comes, whom I shall send to you from the Father, the Spirit of Truth, who proceeds from the Father, He will testify of Me."

Jesus said He is going to send the Helper. If we are going to follow Him in His commandments, we are to receive this Helper.

POWER FOR THE WORK

As Jesus continued to teach of the Holy Spirit we read in John 16:8: "And when He has come, He will convict the world of sin, and of righteousness, and of judgment." The Holy Spirit is the one who convicts us of sin. He is the one that we need to have in our lives to convict us of sin and to give us the strength that we need to avoid it. As you can see, the Helper does the work. Not you or I, but the Holy Spirit.

After Jesus was resurrected, He again told of the promise of the Holy Spirit: "And being assembled together with them, He commanded them not to depart from Jerusalem, but to wait for the Promise of the Father, "which," He said, "you have heard from Me" (Acts 1:4). Jesus was not just suggesting that they get the Holy Spirit—He *commanded* them to wait for Him.

Jesus told them that the Holy Spirit would come soon: ". . . for John truly baptized with water, but you shall be baptized with the Holy Spirit not many days from now" (Acts 1:5). Then Jesus explained the purpose of the baptism of the Holy Spirit: "But you shall receive power when the Holy Ghost has come upon you; and you shall be witnesses to Me in Jerusalem, and in all Judea and Samaria, and to the end of the earth" (Acts 1:8). We need the power to accomplish the tasks He has set forth for us to do.

We read about the Day of Pentecost in the next chapter of Acts 2:14. The word *Pentecost* means "the fiftieth day" and that is when the Promise of the Father, as Jesus called it, came. That is the very reason it is called the Pentecostal experience or, stated another way, the experience of the fiftieth day. That is when the Helper came, and it is easy to see that He really helped Peter. Peter, in his own power, had denied Jesus when the pressure was on but look what he did under pressure *after* receiving the Holy Spirit: "But Peter, standing up with the eleven, raised his voice and said to them, 'Men of Judea and all who dwell in Jerusalem, let this be known to you, and heed my words'" (Acts 2:14). He was no longer shy, or holding back, but came on strong in authority, regardless of what the consequence might be.

Peter continued to preach: "For these are not drunk, as you suppose, since it is only the third hour of the day [9 A.M.]. But this is what was spoken by the prophet Joel . . ."

How about that? Remember when Jesus was talking with the two disciples on the road to Emmaus, He said: "O foolish ones, and slow of heart to believe in all that the prophets have spoken!" (Luke 24:25). Now it seems that Peter is no longer "slow to believe in what the prophets have spoken."

Peter then quoted Joel 2:28–29: "And it shall come to pass in the last days, says God, that I will pour out of My Spirit on all flesh; your sons and your daughters shall prophesy, your young men shall see visions, your old men shall dream dreams. And on My menservants and on My maidservants I will pour out My Spirit in those days; and they shall prophesy."

The Old Testament prophets spoke of what was to come, and Jesus came and fulfilled all those things. Then Jesus prophesied of the coming of the Helper, and He came, fulfilling more prophecy, just as God Himself had planned it. He does the planning, and it is up to each of us to follow through on His plan.

THE PROMISE IS FOR TODAY

Some people have said that the Day of Pentecost was only an event that passed away when the apostles all passed away and that the experience is not for today. But Acts 2:39 says: "For the promise is to you and to your children, and to all who are afar off, as many as the Lord our God will call."

According to that, the promise was to all who heard, and also to their children, and to all who are afar off, and that is to each of us, who are in future generations, for God is still calling us to Himself. It did not die out with the Old Testament apostles. It is still alive today, for you and I are the children of God for He ordained it so. Are you saved? If you are saved, then you have been called! If you are called by God, then this promise is for you!

I have found that there are four basic reasons that Christians have not received the baptism in the Holy Spirit.

1. Lack of salvation, or at least the heart is not right with the Lord. When the church leaders heard that the people of Samaria had received the Word of God, they sent Peter and John to pray for them to receive the baptism in the Holy Spirit. Then a man named Simon tried to buy the power he witnessed as the people received.

Peter rebuked him: "You have neither part nor portion in this matter, for your heart is not right in the sight of God. Repent therefore of this your wickedness, and pray God if perhaps the thought of your heart may be forgiven you. For I see that you are poisoned by bitterness and bound by iniquity" (Acts 8:21).

If your heart is not right with God, you must repent, receive forgiveness from God, and have a clean vessel. Once you are right with God, then the next step is to receive the baptism in the Holy Spirit.

190

2. Lack of knowledge about the baptism of the Holy Spirit. We read in Acts that Paul come to Ephesus and asked the people there, "Did you receive the Holy Spirit when you believed?" They replied, "We have not so much as heard whether there is a Holy Spirit" (Acts 19:2). Many Christians today also do not know of the baptism in the Holy Spirit.

Paul asked, "Into what then were you baptized?" and they said, "Into John's baptism." Then Paul said, "John indeed baptized with a baptism of repentance, saying to the people that they should believe on Him who would come after him, that is, on Christ Jesus." After Paul laid hands on them, the Holy Spirit came upon them, and they spoke with tongues and prophesied (Acts 19:1–7).

3. Being lukewarm. Revelations 3:16 says, "So then, because you are lukewarm, and neither cold nor hot, I will vomit you out of My mouth." Do you fit in this category? My answer to lukewarmness is found in Ephesians 5:17–18: "Therefore do not be unwise, but understand what the will of the Lord is. And do not be drunk with wine, in which is dissipation; but be filled with the Spirit." This tells us it is the will of the Father God that we be filled with the Holy Spirit!

4. Need to exercise more faith. Let's look in Galatians 3:13–14: "Christ has redeemed us from the curse of the law . . . that we might receive the promise of the Spirit through faith." It is necessary to exercise faith to receive the baptism in the Holy Spirit.

The Bible also tells us that we are saved by faith.

> For by grace you have been saved through faith,
> and that not of yourselves; it is the gift of God.
> —EPHESIANS 2:8

The faith that you have is the gift of God.

THE HOLY SPIRIT'S FIRE

John the Baptist said that Jesus would baptize with the Holy Spirit and fire (Luke 3:16). Paul said the will of the Lord is for us to be filled with the Spirit (Eph. 5:18).

If Jesus baptizes us with the Holy Spirit and fire (and He does according to Luke 3:16), then I think it is up to us to keep the fire going. We are told in 2 Timothy 1:6, "For this reason I remind you to fan into flame the gift of God, which is in you through the laying on of my hands" (NIV). Paul says we are to "fan the flame," much the same as old-time blacksmiths used their bellows to increase the heat on their forges. Even today, some of us have bellows by our fireplaces and when the fire begins to get low we pick up the bellows and pump it a few times, aiming it toward the dying embers in the fireplace, and immediately the fire begins to blaze again.

We are told in 1 Thessalonians 5:19: "Do not quench the Spirit." The word *quench* in the original Greek is *sbennumi,* which means "to extinguish or put out." With this in mind, I would say the best translation of this verse would be: Do not put out the Spirit's fire!" I like that because it sounds more like what God had in mind for us. Jesus is the Baptizer, for He baptizes us in the Holy Spirit and fire, and then it is up to us to fan that flame and keep it hot, and never put that fire out, or even so much as suppress it.

In Hebrews 12:29, the Bible says, "For our God is a consuming fire," and that is what He wants to be in our lives. If this becomes reality, then it will truly change your life.

Our Testimony
by George W. Clouse

Mary Jo and I were married in 1969, neither of us being saved, and both of us having had previous marriages. We had lived very worldly lives and thought we were too smart to get caught up in any "religious circles," as we called them. In less than two years God had moved powerfully in our lives and we both received Jesus as our personal Savior. We have never been the same since.

God did many things in our lives during the first year after our salvation. Each of us ministered whenever and wherever opportunities came. We hungered for God and wanted to see Him move in miraculous ways. Our hunger drove us to the Word, and each of us literally devoured the Bible, many times reading the greater part of the night. We would sit at a table, each sharing with the other what God was showing us from His Word. We gradually began to see that God had changed us mightily when we received salvation but further changing and cleaning up depended upon us. The Bible tells us that salvation is a free gift from the grace of God, but He did not say He would change us into what we should be.

When we read in Malachi 3:6, "I am the Lord, I change not," we realized the He was not going to change. Then we looked in the New Testament and found Hebrews 13:8: "Jesus Christ, the same yesterday, and today, and for ever." We asked each other questions. When we got saved was that as far as it went? Was there more? Would God mature us or would we have to mature ourselves? The more we read the Bible the more convinced we became that we could not sit on our hands and wait for God to do something to us. We had to renew our minds and change our thinking to get in line with His. We were both quite sure that He was the one who had saved us, but after salvation, we needed to renew our minds to think like He does so we could change into His image.

In Romans 8:9, we read: "But ye are not in the flesh, but in the Spirit, if so be that the Spirit of God dwell in you. Now if any man have not the Spirit of Christ, he is none of His." This was a very intriguing scripture. In this one verse God spoke of the Spirit of God as well as the Spirit of Christ. What did He mean and was there a difference in the two?

The next scripture we saw was in 1 Corinthians 2:12: "Now we have received, not the Spirit of the world, but the spirit which is of God, that we might know the things that are freely given to us of God." It seemed to me as if God were telling us that there are three different types of spirits we should be aware of.

As I searched and prayed for an answer I felt that the Lord said that the Spirit of God was the spirit of holiness, that each of us were to live a holy life, set apart for His glory. We have both strived to live holy lives from that day until now.

As I continued my search I concluded that the Spirit of Christ was the spirit of anointing, since Christ means "the Anointed One." I decided that this meant that we were to diligently seek His anointing. To minister in His power and in His will it is necessary to minister in His anointing. That has been the goal we have reached for day by day.

If either the Spirit of God or the Spirit of Christ are missing from our ministry, then there is an opening for the devil to come in and wreck havoc.

The Spirit of the world is obvious. Each day as we go on our way we are faced with the spirit of the world. As we listen to news, it seems that it is all bad. It seems that the whole world is negative and if we are not careful, we too will fall into the trap of thinking negatively. The only way to escape the spirit of the world is to renew, or change, our minds. In Romans 12:2, we read: "Be not conformed to this world, but be ye transformed by the renewing of your mind." The word for *transformed* in the Greek is *metamorphoo,* which refers to the metamorphosis that changes an unsightly caterpillar into a beautiful butterfly. That is the change that I want for my life. I want to be transformed from the Spirit of the world, to the Spirit of God, as well as the Spirit of Christ.

Mary Jo, through constant study of the Word, has changed her life, because of the things she has allowed God to do in her life. As she has searched for holiness by moving in the truths of the Word, she has developed the Spirit of God that continually flows in her life. Through obediently answering the call of God on her life, she has yielded her life to move in the Spirit of Christ, or stated another way, "in the anointing."

Recently she discovered another Scripture that changed her life. Second Chronicles 7:14: "If My people who are called by My name will humble themselves, and pray and seek My face, . . ." The one thought, "seek My face," literally jumped off the page of the Bible to her. Then she read about Moses as he sought God's face, that the glory came on him in Exodus 33:20–23:

> But He said, "You cannot see My face; for no man shall see Me, and live." And the Lord said, "Here is a place by Me, and you shall stand on the rock. So it shall be, while My glory passes by, that I will put you in the cleft of the rock, and will cover you with My hand while I pass by. Then I will take away My hand, and you shall see My back; but My face shall not be seen."

Mary Jo realized this meant that when Moses sought God's face, God revealed to him His glory. Exodus 34:28–29 also states:

> So he was there with the Lord forty days and forty nights; he neither ate bread nor drank water. And He wrote on the tablets the words of the covenant, the Ten Commandments. Now it was so, when Moses came down from Mount Sinai (and the two tablets of the Testimony were in Moses' hand when he came down from the mountain), that Moses did not know that the skin of his face shone while he talked with Him.

Now Mary Jo no longer seeks His hand; instead she seeks His face. She is determined to seek His face so that His glory will also be revealed in her.

During the past year, Mary Jo made a promise to God that she would answer His call and go where and when He said to go. As she has shared her ministry in many parts of the world, Mary Jo gleaned revelation and insight from the Lord. These are the truths she shares in her first book, *Getting Free*.

APPENDIX 2

··

PLENTIFUL FRUITS

*by Donna Cento, my friend and board member
of CRM, Intercessor, who travels with me whenever she can.*

"Plentiful Fruits" is the word that comes to mind in describing Mary Jo during the twenty-plus years I have known her.

Although I had met Mary Jo and George before, my first encounter with her wisdom in the Lord was when I asked her to counsel for some needs in my life. Without knowing anything about my past, she spiritually saw me in a room, sitting in a chair with a man standing next to me. This room was dark and there were closed doors all around the room. In the vision I knew that only one of the doors would be the correct choice, but when I turned to the man, he had disappeared. She then informed me that in my past I felt that men had abandoned me so it was hard for me to trust God because of past experiences with men. I knew she was right.

This pattern started when my father passed away when I was fifteen. We were very close and I felt completely abandoned. In looking at the little I know about the men in my family history, my grandfather's lives stand out the most. My grandfather on my father's side died when my father was a small boy, and my grandfather on my mother's side was an alcoholic and would disappear for days at a time. Premature death and alcoholism still remained in my family.

Even though Mary Jo and I were close at the time, we eventually lost contact for quite a few years when the Clouses moved to another state. After about eight years, they moved back to Orlando. Meanwhile, I had gone through years of turmoil in every area of life, but I began to establish my foundation in Christ when our paths crossed again at Wekiva Assembly of God.

Through the past ten years, she has been such a special friend and has ministered the Word of God into my life on a continual basis. When the spirit of revival hit from Lakeland to Toronto to Pensacola, we were at every meeting possible. We also held prayer meetings in my home. The prayer became so intense one evening we knew something has been "birthed in the spiritual realm." At that time, my three children— two sons and a daughter— did not know the Lord.

It first started with my youngest son, who had back-slidden from God and started taking drugs and became involved in that lifestyle. A "druggy" friend of his, who had come back to the Lord, set up a meeting at a Japanese restaurant. Of course, the purpose of the meeting was to talk to my son about the Lord. Along with this "druggy" friend, a pastor of a local church also was at the restaurant. That was the night that my youngest son came back to the Lord! The pastor told him that within twenty-four hours he must leave where he was living because it was a part of the drug lifestyle. At the time, he was staying with his older brother, my second child.

My youngest son's testimony had an impact on my oldest son's life. A few months later my two close friends and I were at a meeting in Melbourne with a visiting minister from England. After the meeting we stopped to eat at a roadside restaurant, when I received a cell phone call from my daughter, my third child. Her words were terrifying. Her older brother had left "forever" —he left thousands of dollars of drug money at her house and was fleeing from the police and the people with whom he had associated. Keep in mind, I did not have any idea, or rather I would not let myself think, he was a drug dealer. That day I did not know if I would ever see him alive again. After the initial fear hit, the Word of God came forth and was spoken by one of my friends: "the seed of the righteous should be delivered" (Prov. 11:21). On our way home we entered into intercessory prayer. My friend saw a vision of a dark cloud, and the dark cloud totally consumed the earth. Then a brilliant red came down from the sky and totally consumed the darkness, just as if it was the very blood of Jesus that had overcome the darkness of the world and healed the situation. Then the Word of the Lord came from Isaiah 57:18–19, "I have seen his ways, and will heal him; I will also lead him, and restore comforts to him and to his mourners. I create the fruit of the lips; Peace, peace to him who is far off and to him who is near." Says the Lord, "And I will heal him."

I was comforted as we continued our way on back to Orlando. When we returned we discovered that my son had first driven almost to the Georgia state line and then the Lord spoke to him, bringing him back to Orlando to our own church, where he rededicated his life to the Lord that very night. He later enrolled in Brownsville School of Ministry, and recently graduated from the school. He is now embarking on his life's work of serving the Lord. Praise God! He has fulfilled His Word.

Now, as for me, through these years of friendship, prayer and teaching of Mary Jo, the generational curses that plagued my family have been, and are continuing, to be destroyed. My sons are living for the Lord. My destroyed finances are restored, and the peace of God and the knowledge of who He is in my life is real!

DONNA'S SON TELLS HIS SIDE OF THE STORY

At the same time Mom and her friends were interceding for me, I was fleeing to get out of the state before the police, as well as the drug lords, caught up with me. I was headed north on Interstate 75 toward the Georgia state line, just trying to survive, seeing no hope for the future. I began to speculate on what my little brother had been telling me about the Lord as the car roared on in the darkness. Then my own voice startled me as I said, "God, if you want to help me, go ahead." (Even though it was a simple request, God heard it.)

That's when the storm came, and what a storm it was. It rained so hard I could not see behind me or ahead of me, in fact I could barely see to get off the road. I knew I was some forty miles south of the state line and I wanted desperately to get out of state, but the storm was controlling my actions. I could barely see, so I stopped at a motel and asked the desk clerk where I was. "Valdosta," he answered flatly. How could I be in Valdosta, Georgia? I still have no answer of how I could be there.

I secured a room, took a quick shower, and lay on the bed. The Bible on the nightstand was open to Psalms 34–35. I started reading, all the while crying like a baby. I had not cried like that since I was a child, and I did not understand why I was crying. In fact, there were many things I did not understand. I did not understand how I could be in Georgia, because I didn't think I had been driving long enough to be that far north. The mileage and distance did not agree, but I do remember telling God "if You want to help me, go ahead!" The only answer I can come up with is that He must have translated me.

The next morning the television meteorologist was talking about the "freak storm" that came out of nowhere, with no warning. He was saying how this area had not seen one like that ever before.

The next morning I woke up at ten o' clock, and sure enough, I was in Valdosta, Georgia. I went to the police station to see if there was a warrant for my arrest, and there wasn't. I waited around for about an hour and again went back to check at the police station. Again there was nothing, so I decided to go back to Orlando. I started driving down the Interstate, when a van passed me and slammed on the brakes. I immediately drove out around the van, because I recognized tactics of the "druggies." I prayed: "Lord, make them disappear." God told me to look in the rear view mirror to see what He had done. When I looked, there were no tire marks in the grass, no exits off the highway, no place for them to go, and, yet, the van was not there. Another miracle!

That night I went to the evening service at my mom's church. The pastor was on vacation that week and a visiting pastor spoke. The devil tried to tell me that I should not be there because I had sold drugs to these people's kids. I couldn't understand the speaker, but his voice comforted me. He gave the altar call and I went to the front. I couldn't get to him because some of the ladies from the congregation had surrounded him. I dropped to the altar and started weeping profoundly, as one of the associate pastors read Psalms 34–35 to me and prayed for me. This confirmed everything to me. When I got up my whole countenance changed, and the strongman was broken once and for all. Praise God!

Within a few weeks I was on my way to Pensacola to the Brownsville School of Ministry Bible College from where I have since graduated. God has completely reversed the direction of my life to such a degree that when I think back on it, I can scarcely believe it.

Isaiah (53) — By his strips we are healed.

take comunion 1X per week every Sun? —

Deut (28):1-14 —

Daniel (10) — repented for the sins of Israel —

Blessing = lifted up, my life touches others, free of envy and strife (1000 generation)

Curse = reach a pennacle of success and the bottom falls out, dishonor our parents —) to the (4th) generation —